LIVING WITCHERY:
Beginner Witch Guide

Living Witchery: Beginner Witch Guide

Edited by
Alexandra Tanet,
Kim Fairminer &
Sandra Greenhalgh

© copyright Byrning Tyger 2021
Each author is copyright owner of their own contributed materials.

The moral rights of the authors have been asserted.

All rights reserved. Except as permitted under the Australian Copyright Act 1968 (for example, a fair dealing for the purposes of study, research, criticism or review), no part of this book may be reproduced, stored in a retrieval system, communicated or transmitted in any form or by any means without prior written permission.

All inquiries should be made to the Publisher

Printed in Australia
Cover design by Kylie Sek of Cover Culture

Disclaimer

Views or opinions represented in this publication are personal and belong solely to the individual author. Although the editors and publisher have made every effort to ensure that the information in this book was correct at press time, the editor and publisher do not assume and hereby disclaim any liability to any party for any loss, damage, or disruption caused by errors or omissions, whether such errors or omissions result from negligence, accident, or any other cause.

Some names and identifying details have been changed to protect the privacy of individuals.

ISBN 978-0-6482701-4-0

www.byrningtyger.com

In the spirit of reconciliation, we acknowledge the Traditional Custodians of Country throughout Australia and their connections to land, sea, sky and community. We pay our respects to Elders past and present and future.

Table of Contents

- Introduction 1
- Beginner Witch Reality Check 2
- **FORMING: The What and Where** **3**
  - Witchcraft in Australia 5
  - Reconciling Witchcraft 10
  - Labels, Terms and Concepts 18
  - Covens and Study Groups 21
- **FUNDAMENTALS: Starting Points** **23**
  - Ethics 25
  - Meditation 28
  - The Inner Planes 35
  - Spirit Guides 37
  - Energy Sensing, Auras and Chakras 39
  - Grounding, Centering, and Protection 43
  - Reincarnation 45
  - Coming Out of the Broom Closet 47
- **FOUNDATIONS: Build Your Practice** **49**
  - Book of Shadows 51
  - Your Personal Altar 53
  - Correspondences, Elements and Elementals 55
  - The Witch's Tools 61
    - Athame 62
    - Wand 62
    - Chalice 63
    - Pentacle 63
    - Other magical tools 64
  - Consecration Ritual 66
  - The Wheel of the Year in the Southern Hemisphere 68
    - Samhain 70
    - Yule 71
    - Imbolc 72
    - Ostara 73
    - Beltane 74
    - Litha 75
    - Lughnasadh 76

Mabon 77
Deity: Goddess, God and the Gods 78
How to Connect with a Patron Deity 83
FACETS: Witchery Lore **87**
  Sky Yarning – Indigenous Astronomy 89
  The Magic of Time 93
    Moon cycles 99
    Planetary magic 101
  Bringing Magick into Everyday Life 105
    Travel magick 111
  A Witch's Apothecary 115
    Apothecary basics 120
    Vitality oil 122
    Persephone loose incense 124
    Ritual body scrub 125
  Crystals and Earth Magic 126
    Charging and cleansing your crystals 129
    Commonly used crystals 130
    Creating crystal grids 136
  I've Been Hexed or Cursed. Please Help! 139
  Energetic Cleansing 142
    Space cleansing ritual 143
    Suggestions for smoke cleansing 147
  Divination 151
    Divination tools 153
FESTIVALS: Rituals and Ceremonies **157**
  Crafting a Solitary or Small Group Ritual 159
  The Altar 161
  Public or Large Group Rituals 164
  Walking the Wheel of the Year 166
FOCUS: Magick and Spellwork **177**
  Magick – Tips and Techniques 179
    Magick and spellwork tips 180
    Magical power 181
  Raising Energy with Sound and Movement 183
  Spellwork Step-by-Step 188
  Colour Correspondences 190
  Candle Magick 191
    Dressing a candle 192
  Spell Bottles 194
    House protection spell bottle 194
    Money spell bottle 196
  Spell Boxes 197

- Love spell box........197
- Charm Bags........199
- Amulets and Talismans........201
- Sweetening-up Spell........203
- Freezer Spell........205
- **FLOURISH: The Circle Coven Tradition 207**
  - What is The Circle Coven?........209
    - Our Probationary Novice (ProbNov) program........212
    - Rites of passage – Dedication and Initiation........214
  - Preparing for Ritual........216
    - Ritual clothing........216
    - Getting ready........218
  - Circle Coven Ritual........220
    - Circle casting........221
    - Quarters........223
    - Invocation and evocation........224
- References and Bibliography........231
- Additional Resources for Further Study........232
- Acknowledgements and Credits........233
- Biographies........235

Introduction

Living Witchery: Beginner Witch Guide is a magical cauldron that combines wisdom from a variety of authors. The main ingredients are teaching materials from The Circle Coven, re-written by me and co-edited by Kim Fairminer and Sandra Greenhalgh. At times, it's difficult to know exactly who said or wrote what, as we've created such a delightfully blended elixir.

Added to this potent mix are chapters by selected guest authors. These practitioners share their unique and varied personal experiences of living witchery. Topics such as Indigenous astronomy, herbal lore, tips for everyday magic, crystals, walking meditations for seasonal celebrations and house cleansing add wonderful highlights to the brew.

All authors live in Australia. As much as possible, we have contextualised our witchcraft practices to the wonderful land we call home.

Bright blessings,
Alexandra Tanet

Witchcraft is a transformative practice.
We change, and everything else changes around us.
This process is continuous, though at times we may not be fully aware of what is happening or why it is occurring.
Witchcraft helps us to understand.

Beginner Witch Reality Check

You don't have to buy expensive things to be a witch.
You don't have to dress a certain way to be a witch.
Meditate, meditate, meditate.
Spend as much time in nature as you can.
Read as much as you can.
Try to validate your inner world experiences with what is happening in the outer worlds.
Honey catches more flies than vinegar. A bit of kindness goes a long way.
As much as possible, use ethically sourced products.
Learn the fundamentals before doing spellwork.
Don't automatically assume a spell is needed every time you feel annoyed, frustrated or ill.
Have a flexible mind. Over time, things can and do change – particularly your perceptions.
Intent isn't everything. It's **one** *of the things.*
Embrace the journey.

FORMING: The What and Where

Let's get started!

Embrace concepts you feel comfortable with, and temporarily park to one side those that don't align with your current values and beliefs.
Things change over time; you may find yourself back where you first began, seeing the same things with a fresh perspective.

Witchcraft in Australia

The focus of this book is modern witchcraft derived from practices that originated in the British Isles and western Europe. This flavour of witchcraft has been shaped by a wide range of influences, including ancient Greek, Roman and Egyptian civilisations. Some Victorian-era magical groups also integrated Eastern spiritual concepts into their ceremonial magick practices, and these have flowed into our form of contemporary witchcraft.

There are minimal barriers to learning this inclusive Western style of witchcraft. You do not need to live in a specific location or be of a particular gender, body shape, skin colour or race. Contemporary witchcraft is flexible and dynamic. We don't have one true leader to decry: *"Thou must do this, or you are not a witch!"*

Witches living in Australia, particularly those with a Western cultural orientation, experience a unique set of circumstances due to the country's history and geographical location. We inhabit a land where Aboriginal and Torres Strait Islander peoples have lived for over 50,000 years. Consequently, non-First Nations people need to be as culturally sensitive as possible. The flora and fauna of Australia also differs significantly from that of Europe. Non-native plant and animal species have been introduced, often with terrible consequences. And of course, we are 'down under' in Australia as we are located south of the equator. Our seasons do not align with northern hemisphere seasons, and our moon phases also look different.

For all these reasons, some British Isles and European texts or practices just don't make a lot of sense when you live in Australia. What are we to do?

Witches in Australia are fortunate because we have opportunities to create our own new ways. We are able to valiantly explore and innovate. Rather than struggle with European-centric texts, engage with what is around you – plants, animals, people, land, local spirits – and joyously activate your curiosity. Here are some practical examples to help you create satisfying and meaningful witchery practices, regardless of where you live in Australia.

The seasons

Observe local seasonal variations. Over the course of a year, keep a diary of weather patterns such as temperature, winds, rain, or snow. Make notations about your emotions, or what is happening in your personal lifecycle at the same time. You may like to compare your diary with historical records, to evaluate changes or similarities over the decades. As part of your seasonal studies, try to include records of locally grown fruit, grain and vegetables, observing when they are planted and harvested.

Your local seasons are unlikely to neatly align with the temperate northern hemisphere cycle of Spring, Summer, Autumn, Winter. And of course, due to the large size of the Australian continent, there are many seasonal variations. Subtropical Brisbane, for example, is different to tropical Darwin, which is different to temperate Hobart. That's why it's best to pay keen attention to your local environment. Learn about where you live.

Plants

Notice the plants around you. You might like to focus on those growing in your own neighbourhood, or instead choose a specific bushland or nearby park. It's amazing how much you can learn about the common and botanical names of the plants and trees by using books, electronic apps, or asking local gardeners.

Take your time and study plants as they go through their seasonal changes. You may notice that some changes require external stimulation such as fire or cold weather. At what time of year does the plant shed their leaves or bark? When does it flower? How do the flowers smell when in full bloom? How large do trees grow? Can you find stories about local native plants and their properties?

Don't forget to include introduced species as well as native plants in your study, as these too make up your surroundings. There is an abundance of European lore associated with trees such as oak, yew, birch and willow. Learn which of the introduced species are considered noxious weeds, such as groundsel and lantana. Many townships have programs where you can volunteer to remove invasive plants from waterways or public spaces, and replace them with native trees and bushes. These wonderful initiatives allow you to connect and give back to the earth in a positive way.

Animals, birds and insects

Consider the living creatures in your surroundings. Even though you may live in an inner-city apartment, there are many animals, birds and critters nearby.

From the ubiquitous crow and magpie through to rare and beautiful kingfishers, we are blessed to have a wealth of bird life around us. Australia seems to be renowned for its deadly or poisonous animal inhabitants, but aside from crocodiles, there are no large, free-roaming land predators such as bears or wolves.

As with the previous exercises, take time to raise your awareness, improve your knowledge and consider the creatures you share space with. How do their appearance and life cycles vary? What are their habits and preferred habitats? For example, the oft-scorned ibis is truly majestic in full flight over rural countryside, far from urban parks and rubbish bins.

There is so much magick to be found by studying native animals, as well as those within your dwelling. Companion animals such as cats and dogs, who share our homes, hold a special place in our hearts. The cat has a long history of being a witch's supernatural companion and for good reason, given their otherworldly attributes.

Solar connections

Make a simple sun dial. Tape a piece of paper to a flat surface in a location that receives full sunlight throughout the day. Then add an upright item, such as a straight stick, to the middle of the paper. During the day, every hour or half-hour, draw a line where the shadow falls, and mark it with the time. This is a useful way to connect with your local circadian rhythms.

Over the course of a year, track the movement of the rising and setting sun as it movies southward and northward across the horizon, while you stay in the same location. An easy way to do this is to take a photo of the sunset or sunrise once a month to monitor seasonal movements.

Lunar connections

Observe the waxing and waning of the moon. The appearance of the moon in the southern hemisphere differs to the northern hemisphere. See how the shape of the moon changes over time.

Draw the appearance of the moon on a large piece of paper, over one moon cycle. If you are unable to go outside, or visibility is poor, you can use a 'live tracker' app on your smart phone or computer and watch the moon that way.

The new/crescent moon is visible on the western horizon soon after sunset. At the first quarter, the moon rises in the East at noon and is directly overhead at sunset. The full moon rises on the eastern horizon at sunset. In the waning half of the cycle, you will need to stay up later and later to see the moon rise in the East. By the balsamic phase (the very end of the waning phase, as the moon becomes dark) you can only see the moon in the East just before dawn.

For an in-depth exploration of the lunar cycles, and how to weave them into your life and practice of witchcraft, see *The Magic of Time* chapter.

Historical connections

The *Reconciling Witchcraft* chapter includes specific recommendations to engage sensitively with Australian First Nations peoples' history and culture. Here are some other ideas which may help.

Learn about the history of your surroundings. This can be fascinating as well as potentially confronting, as the prevailing narrative might mask a traumatic history. The various Boundary Streets within Brisbane are local examples. These seemingly innocently named streets originally marked the boundaries of racially segregated curfews. Another activity is to learn the name/s of the First Nations peoples from your area (if you haven't already done this) and discover their words for the places where you live or work.

To find out more about your local history, a Google search is of course an easy option, but it's certainly not the only one. Learn from the people in your community. Are there local (formal or informal) historians you can speak with? State library archives have pre-recorded histories from early colonial settlers, immigrants from other countries, or elderly local people. Are there independently produced books in your local shops or library? If your ancestors were born in a different country, you may like to track their travels, from their arrival point in Australia through to where they used to live.

Genius Loci

As you explore your environment, and become in-tune with your surroundings, you will connect with the Genius Loci, or 'spirit of place'. This is a special place or space where you feel an immense sense of connection. Perhaps you feel uplifted, nurtured or protected. Perhaps you get tingles all over your body, or have a sensation of the otherworlds or magick seeping through, enabling you to glimpse daemons or fairies or gods. These are the places that sing to the mysteries within your soul.

You likely already have experienced Genius Loci in wild, natural places such as waterfalls, on mountain tops or by the ocean. However, it could be a certain tree, or a bend by the local creek, which has no outward specialness, but holds particular relevance to you. Spend time there to meditate or do personal rituals, if that is appropriate. You can give offerings of stories, poetry or libations of milk and honey. Please don't leave the stubs of candles, or physical remains of non-organic offerings in public spaces; that's magical vandalism.

The reason some physical places speak with us on an intuitive level can be attributed to phenomenon like ley lines or Earth energies. Regardless of the reasons, we just know on a deeper level there is something different about certain places. So, if you are not already aware of places in your environment with a powerful spirit of place, then take the time to walk slowly where you live, paying attention to how your body and psyche are responding to what's around you.

Slow down. Be quiet. Breathe deeply. Listen. And be respectful.

Reconciling Witchcraft

By Chadrac Sloane

I am Chadrac. I am 40-something years old, a mother of four, a grandmother to one, and related to many more that are of kin. I am genetically of mixed descent, mostly Irish, British, and Indigenous Australian heritage (that I know of). I am a proud Barkindji woman and my family is blessed to have remained connected to culture. I was born in a town on the top of the Great Dividing Range in northern New South Wales on what is known as the Northern Tablelands. Indigenous nations of this region include the Kamilaroi (Gomeroi), Anaiwan, Ngarabal, and Banbai. Many Indigenous groups and nations have used this region over thousands of years and their people still live in and around the Northern Tablelands today.

I grew up living with my grandparents and with my mother, who was quite young and very brave to rear me as a single mother in those times. I am grateful for my upbringing and how it has shaped my path. I spent my entire childhood on top of those mountains, and they have never stopped calling me back. Those mountains taught me so much about life and about magic. Now I am based in the western side of the Kulin nations in Wathaurong (Wadda Wurrung) Country. I am a student of, and a worshipper of, nature.

As a teenager, I thought it was all very hard and particularly strict living with my grandparents, but now I would not change a thing; it was a true blessing. I had to chop wood to cook dinner and heat water for washing as we did not have mains gas, power, or sewage. It was strict because it had to be. If the chores were not done, there were repercussions far beyond that which implicated me alone. The consequences affected everyone. The conveniences that many take for granted these days were not so common in days gone by. I look back upon my childhood with nostalgia, as it was of a time before.

I learned old ways that other children my age were not learning. I did not have the flash new Nintendo or Atari of the day – but I did know how to grow, catch, and gather my own resources to prepare my own meals. I was shown and taught how to make a shelter without a hammer and to tell the time without a watch. I grew up learning a craft, and that craft is a way of life. To know how to be in the bush, to be an actual part of the country, and to hear the messages that are being told to you. To hear the stories and be able to clearly see the lessons. To know and to be part of Country and not just on it. These teachings will never leave me. I am blessed to have passed them onto my children, as they will pass them onto theirs. This is the rock-solid foundation upon which my daily spiritual practice is formed.

I was born and grew up on the lands of the Anaiwan, Kwaimbul and Banbai people. Before the 1830s, these groups lived in and moved through the area. These people used the country for camping, for fishing and for hunting alongside the wetlands that are now known as the Mother of Ducks Lagoon in a small town called Guyra. This lagoon is a large stretch of water that is fourteen kilometres in circumference. The water is held in a stilted volcanic crater, part of the volcanic system that created the Great Dividing Range as we see it as today.

There are differing translations of the word Guyra, what it stands for and means. As with the whole continent, differences come from people within the various language groups who traditionally lived in these districts. Guyra is said to originate from the language of the Anaiwan people, meaning 'white cockatoo' or 'fishing place'. Another translation from the language of the Gumbayniggir people, who lived on the eastern seaboard side of the Great Dividing Range, tells us that Guyra means 'black cockatoo'.

All these people were adept hunters. They compromised with the harsh winter climate by wearing furs and pelts. They knew where and how to move through the country with little or no ecological impact and would thrive in each season. In the 1830s, Europeans colonised the area. This region is now known for its wool, lamb and potatoes in the towns of Armidale, Guyra, and Glen Innes in the northern New England region. I have a connection to this Country and this place, yet it is not the place of my blood heritage.

This is a pertinent point for many Australians who are on a spiritual path, including Australian witches. I hear this mentioned often, as if it is barrier to one's ability to connect. The attitude "oh, but I am not from this country" is not a perspective that can aid you in a spiritual life. We are all part of one world, the one universe, for we are it and it is us. I raise this as a point of contention because there is widespread misconception that a person's specific location and sense of place is of relevance to daily practice. The country upon which I was born and where I learned to be me is far from the lands of my mother's bloodline; my maternal grandfather's lineage is from the Djabb-wurrung and Barkindji people of Victoria.

Sanctioned dispossession and displacement have determined that many Indigenous Australians are no longer on their traditional home or bloodline lands. They too are immigrants to a country that is not theirs by lineage. But as Indigenous people travel the country, we all still practice cultural and spiritual protocols and respect the people and Country upon where we reside. It is all still one country, one cosmos and the same life force. I share this in the hope that it can help you – with heritage from across the wide oceans – to connect with this country in a more valuable and meaningful way.

Protocols are followed when travelling. As we move across the land, we acknowledge the Countries, and the people. There are rituals that are done when welcoming and farewelling people onto Country. It is important to note that not just anyone can perform what is known as a Welcome to Country Ceremony. For this ceremony to be performed, it must be an Elder from the nations upon which you are located who welcomes you to their Country. That is not a role for anyone else to fill. There is however space for an Acknowledgement of Country. This can be performed by anyone, but only if it is done in a respectful and honourable manner.

To perform this ritual, you must acknowledge and pay respect to the past, the present and the future Traditional Custodians and Elders of the nation and clans upon where you walk on that day. You must honour the continuation of cultural, spiritual, and educational practices of the First Nations peoples. The following text can be adapted to include the nation and clan/language groups for your area or more emotive words if you feel called to do so:

'In the spirit of reconciliation, I acknowledge the Traditional Custodians of the Country throughout this Country and their connections to sky, land, sea and community. We pay our respect to their Elders, past, and present, and extend that respect to all the future traditional custodians of the Country here in this time and place today'.

When you come to sit at any place of Country, the first thing you are going to do is to just sit and you are going to speak to and listen to all the spirits of that Country. There are rock spirits, tree spirits, grass spirits, insect spirits, birds, mammals, fish, invertebrates. All these living things have their own individual spirit, and we must pay respects to those. We must acknowledge that every single one of those spirits is just as important as our own spirit and without them our spirit is nothing. We are not going to just speak to them though; we are also going to listen and listen very carefully to what those spirits have to say.

In addition to using the appropriate words of acknowledgement, it is important to acknowledge the use of plants and herbs when you are performing rituals. Questions to ask yourself are:
- Have I considered the history behind the plants I have chosen for my work?
- Have I considered using native plants that are in abundance across my biosphere?
- What is on the ground and being offered near me?

Eucalyptus has been used for generations here for cleansing and clearing and for communication with the spirits of the Dreaming. The use of plants that are not native to the Country is as offensive as the use of an imported ritual on sacred lands. It is perfectly ok to use a few fallen gum leaves that have blown across your path on your afternoon walk. Spirit has blown them to you for a reason. Take these gifts and use them in your craft.

A few eucalyptus leaves make cute little besoms for sweeping and clearing. You can also use crushed gum leaf as a loose incense blend, just as you would any other herb (for example, rosemary); it works very effectively. Please do not strip trees for their leaves. This is unnecessary and wasteful. Use your observation skills in nature; take note of the things on the ground first and you will realise why it is inappropriate to strip the trees.

The value that Indigenous Australians place on natural resources stems from traditional histories and the strong relationship to and respect for the land. Indigenous Australians use the natural resources according to Lore, Lore that has been passed down through the generations orally and recorded in art and stone constructions. For the Indigenous community, spiritual beliefs are not separated from the everyday, like you may see in Westernised societies (for example, working from nine to five and leaving your spirituality for church on Sunday). This type of separative lifestyle is far detached from the holistic and all-encompassing way of life that Indigenous Australians are taught and shown.

The stories, the Dreaming and the Lore are established in a way that defines people as the custodians of the land, sea and sky and it is hence our responsibility to maintain the systems and various species. Ultimately the health of the land, the maintenance of biodiversity and the stability of the ecosystems is deeply entwined and linked into the wellbeing of all people, both in the corporeal sense and in the spiritual realm.

Australian Indigenous cultures are knowledgeable in the connections that exist between the night sky, terrestrial land (earthy realm) and the sub-terrains below (underworld) and how these are vital parts of all existence. The night sky and its cosmic landscape plays a significant role in the ordering of all things and acts as a type of agenda or calendar of sorts for human life. There are visible changes in the night sky that are the same every year and are visible at every important season. The movement of planets and constellations tells stories and shows the Lore. In some cases, as recorded in ancient cave paintings, the night sky reflects the terrestrial movements of people and animals. These observations reinforce the holistic approach to spirituality and shows us how the night sky of the cosmos was and still is an important part of the Indigenous landscape. The skyworld is explored more in the *Sky Yarning Indigenous Astronomy* chapter.

I began by looking into spirituality, and more specifically, occultism, mythology, and witchcraft at the local library. In the beginning, I struggled with the various definitions and labels. Truth be told, not much has changed regarding my thoughts on labels and how they are used. They tend to move with the trends and times. It was not just definitions and labels that troubled me, but also the texts themselves.

There is an abundance of books written by Western white males about spirituality and the craft; whereas the types of craft and nature-based skills I was familiar with were not documented. Nor could I find anything of relevance in the library catalogue (for those of us old enough to remember using a cardboard catalogue drawer). This led me to dive deeper into academic tablatures and ancient transcripts, where I discovered the concept of the anima mundi and many other fabulous and fascinating myths, stories, and beliefs that resonated with me from across the globe.

Through this research, I saw that there are familiar patterns within nature worship and witchcraft; most have quite similar collaborative beliefs and systems of practice. The use of sound, beats, dance, and circular rituals is similar across cultures. The recognition of natural places of power, divinity, and cosmic activity is another recurring theme. Across the globe, many human civilisations continue to worship natural forces. You can even see common themes repeated between the deities, saints, gods and archetypes from many countries and cultures of origin. Just as there is incredible diversity in spiritual expression throughout history, across the world, there is also incredible diversity across Indigenous Australia.

I have included suggestions for seeking acknowledgment from the Traditional Owners and guardians of the Country upon which you reside. This will vary across the country, just as it does across the world, as there are over 200 nations and clans, with each individual nation having individual terrain and subsequently language groupings with relevant Dreaming stories. These differences, though vast, are also threaded with similarities; the basics, such as respect, honesty, trust, and reliability, speak louder than any words you may ever mumble. Your actions and choices in life will determine your ability to connect with the land on which you live.

It is also important to note that this great land has been the location of historical atrocities, some that have never been spoken of or yet acknowledged. Additionally, since the beginning of time, there have always been some places and Country that should not ever be interfered with; do not attempt to start discourse with the spirits in such places. Some Countries have had recent trauma and that Country too, is not to be inhabited. There are some cases on Country where we must just let things be; as it is not our place to be trying to fix, cleanse or bless anything. Leave it and respectfully walk away.

As you meander down your own spiritual path, you will meet with challenges being a witch in Australia. It is not an easy path, but it is a rewarding one. There are many considerations as you seek the balance between living an urban lifestyle and measuring the impact that your life has on the environment. Think about your agricultural footprint. How far, wide and reaching is your supply chain for food and produce? Living the life of a modern nature-based worshipper is a challenge in modern times; balance is vital to so many things and crucial to magical workings.

Social and political events across the country and world also contribute to one's spiritual work. I am a firm believer in the balance of dark and light, life and death. Living life in a modern multicultural country is a blessing on one hand, and on the other it can also be a path filled with winding bends and treacherous potholes. This duality is an unavoidable part of living a domesticated human existence, and it also shapes my eclectic practice.

These are unavoidable tensions, and anyone who is in touch with their own animality and spirituality will attest to the frustrations of this dichotomy. The internal monologue and personal battle to fight the pull to change your lifestyle goes deeper than many of us realise. It is a primordial instinctual drive to take the spiritual path – but then there is also societal conditioning and imprinting; the earthy pulls of finance, food and rent that make this path a challenge on various levels. The types of barriers depend on your individual circumstances.

There are two heavy weights that bear on the scales of the modern witch. One is to want to go fully 'off the grid', to be self-sufficient and to be able to practice magick as a part of that holistic lifestyle and to be at one with nature and with spirit and to just be. This step is quite large, as it also involves having the ability to pull back wholly from mainstream society. Let us not forget the institutions that must be dealt with, such as currency, laws and, of course, taxes. The off-the-grid concept is also quite a utopian perspective which makes this goal unattainable for most.

And on the other side of the scales, tipping that weight, there are the societal pressures to get an education and have a successful career – as some witches like to call it, their 'muggle' jobs. To go out into the world and contribute for a wage. The scales of the natural and historically traditional lifestyles weigh on one side and, on the other, there are the pressures of Westernised modern-day life.

It is possible to find a balance in your spiritual practice. It is up to you where and when you choose to start taking steps and making changes in your thinking, choices, and actions. It really does come down to small acts in everyday life. The simple acts that some people like to term 'mundane' can have the greatest magical impact of all. Ecological choices, like having a compost bin, reconsidering your use of public landfill, and paying it forward where you can. These are also mindful acts that can help to restore the natural balance and order of things.

Of course, a lot more can be done. Corporeal mindful acts are just as magical as the acts of an elaborately planned grand ritual. For example, making the choice to replant native plants and shrubs over introduced and ornamental species helps to restore the natural balance of things, alongside the benefits of aiding the native wildlife to remain established with their intended diet. The birds, the native bees and the plants have a tight ecological and spiritual relationship, and that cycle needs support, particularly in urban and heavily farmed areas. These acts of botanical restoration and reconciliation are magick in themselves, and a magick that you can watch grow and bloom, season after season. These acts of ecological service also teach spiritual lessons – after you have initially mindfully planted them, you can then observe and learn from the plants. A relationship develops which could potentially lead to you being able to consensually work with that plant's energies.

The many dualisms of Australian culture are complex enough on their own without incorporating the concepts of craft and magick into it. The effects the new colonial culture has had on nature-based belief practices and Indigenous people and cultures must be remembered. Much has been lost at the intersection where several cultures have collided. In the spirit of reconciliation, there is hope that nature-based ideologies can be restored and finally revered with the sacredness that they deserve.

Connecting to your country – observations and acknowledgements

Here is a short list of activities to help you develop your understanding and bond with the country you inhabit:

- Observe land structures and geological landforms. Acknowledge the male and female landforms. See how the breast-shaped hills equate to female places of Country and phallus-shaped to male.
- See the universe as one whole being and not separate entities.
- Focus on the cohesive energies that are universal and all-knowing.
- Understand that all living things have and are spirit.
- Contact your local Land Council or local Aboriginal Corporation or meeting place for more advice about acknowledging Traditional Owners in your area.

Online resources for finding Country and language groups

Gambay

Gambay is a map of Australia's first languages. It showcases over 780 languages, using data contributed by regional language centres and programs working directly with language communities around Australia.
<www.abc.net.au/indigenous/features/gambay-languages-map>

AIATSIS – Map of Indigenous Australia

This site includes maps of First Nations Country. Note that the borders between groups are purposefully represented as slightly blurred and are by no means exact, nor will they ever be. Some of the information shown on the map is still contested by First Nations groups and some organisations, and may not be agreed to by some traditional custodians. Note that the Westernised land ownership concept, as it exists today (for example, the concept of fencing/boundaries) was not the same for Indigenous peoples – hence these maps are just a guide.
<www.aiatsis.gov.au/explore/map-indigenous-australia>

Labels, Terms and Concepts

As humans, we like to define things, to compartmentalise between 'that' and 'not that'. Definitions and labels are useful, as they help us to form shared understandings. Unfortunately, labels also cause difficulties when people ascribe different meanings to the same word.

For this reason, an upfront understanding of witchy labels, terminology (or jargon!) and concepts is vital when you are learning witchcraft. If you are not sure of a word or phrase, or the context, it's best to ask what it means to that person. Doing this can help break down potential barriers, and foster understanding.

Let's explore some common terms and concepts associated with contemporary witchcraft, always being mindful that there is no one way of being a witch. No path is more or less valid that other paths.

Wicca

This is arguably the most debated and misused word in contemporary witchcraft. Within this book, the word Wicca only refers to the Initiatory traditions that predominantly trace lineage to Gerald Gardner (Gardnerian) or Alex Sanders (Alexandrian). For a fantastic contemporary exploration of Wicca, I suggest reading *Traditional Wicca* by Thorn Mooney. If you feel like delving in a bit deeper, *A Witches Bible Compleat* by Stewart and Janet Farrar is recommended as a classic text.

There are a few reasons for the different uses of the word Wicca. One is the 1990s trend to call yourself a 'Wiccan' rather than a witch, as it was more socially acceptable and didn't target you as a potential devil-worshipper. Scott Cunningham's marvellous book *Wicca: Magic for the Solitary Practitioner* also inspires many witches to name themselves as wiccan (with a lowercase w).

A common saying is 'all Wiccans are witches, but not all witches are Wiccan'.

Eclectic

I like to describe eclectic witchcraft as 'anything witchy that works'. By nature, eclectic witchcraft is fluid, flexible and experiential. Eclectic witches don't follow a particular, defined system, but instead blend folk, mythic, and magical sources to create new practices or traditions. However, eclectic witchcraft is not a licence to integrate teachings from closed cultural practices or profit from these.

White vs black witches

It's very simple to split our worldview into two parts – right or wrong, yes or no, us or them, him or her, war or peace, and, of course, black or white witches. But trying to understand life by splitting everything into polar opposites is limiting and flawed.

Commonly, constructive or positive magick is called white magick, while curses, bindings and magick of a destructive or malicious nature are labelled as black magick. These two categories have been extended to include the witches practising such magick. White witches are considered to be life affirming, healing and 'good', in comparison to black witches who are 'evil' and nasty. Despite excellent choices in footwear, evil witches in stories often get squashed under flying houses and are portrayed as the baddies. Bah! Too simple. Too silly. Life's not two dimensional. We exist in a rainbow spectrum of colours.

Try using the words 'benevolent' and 'malevolent' instead of 'black' and 'white' if you feel the need to categorise magick in this way.
It is the will of the person which forms the shape of the magick.

Other types of witchcraft

There are many witchcraft traditions and categories in addition to Wicca or eclectic. Some categories share similar themes, yet are as diverse as the witches who align with them. Here's a snapshot of some frequently used terms:

- ✦ *Green witch.* Loves plants, herb craft, the Earth and nature.
- ✦ *Kitchen witch.* Very practical and likes to use common household items in spellwork. Uses meal preparation and cooking as a form of magick.
- ✦ *Hedge witch.* Traditionally, these were the healers or cunning folk who lived on the outskirts of villages. The title refers to the practice of 'crossing the hedge' to journey to the otherworlds or spirit lands.

- **Faerie witch.** Has a focus on folklore and interacting with the Fae (for example., sprites or fairies).
- **Cosmic witch.** Integrates astrology, astronomy and moon cycles into their practices.
- **Sea witch or water witch.** Has a strong bond with the ocean or water, as well as the weather.
- **Sandwich.** Yes. That's a joke. Sorry for those who dislike puns.
- **Hereditary witch.** Magical practices are passed down via family members through generations. However, this does not mean that witchiness is carried in bloodlines…and you certainly don't need to be born into a family of witches to be a witch!

My friend Tess advises:

'Of course, there's no need to narrow yourself down to being one type or another, but some people will find their focus resides almost entirely within one of these categories. By the same token, many will identify with certain aspects of a lot of them. Beginners need some reassurance that there's no need to get too hung up on labels or categories.'

Spiritual vs religious

At times, witches will state they are 'spiritual but not religious'. This differentiation is important because while organised religion requires adherence to rigid structures and a set belief system, witchcraft certainly does not. Spirituality relates to the individual's internal state of being, rather than to an external establishment. Having said that, this division is not absolute, as some witchcraft traditions are legally recognised religious entities.

Atheist/agnostic/animist witches

Not all witches integrate deity (gods or goddesses or a 'greater spirit') into their practice. Instead, some prefer to link with archetypes, ancestral spirits or nature spirits. Other witches have a secular or atheist practice, rather than a focus on spirituality. I guess the main thing here is not to make assumptions about someone else's practice, as not all witches follow the same path.

Covens and Study Groups

A coven is formed by two or more people who practice a common theme of witchcraft. Although this book is heavily influenced by coven practice, most Australian witches will never have the opportunity to join an established coven, and some don't ever want to join one. A witch who practices alone is called a 'solitary'. The plural is 'solitaries'. Solitaire, on the other hand, is a card game, rather than a descriptor for a witch who is not a member of a group or coven.

Traditionally, there is a maximum of thirteen witches in a coven. Apart from magical traditions and lore linked to the number thirteen, common sense reasons – such as how many witches can you fit into a small room – may dictate the number of coven members. Modern day covens can be as large or as small as they want to be. Some contemporary witches belong to online covens and are perfectly content with that option.

Pronounce the word 'coven' like 'oven' ("cuv-en"), not like 'over' ("coh-ven").

Why join a coven?

Magical and spiritual processes are accelerated and influenced by coven membership. Ongoing, close interactions with other witches is, of course, the major difference between covencraft and solitary practice. Yes, working with a coven can be confronting, difficult and disturbing. As Jean-Paul Sartre wrote, 'Hell is other people'. Challenges are multiplied when you are a member of a magical group. It is easier to feel uber spiritual and achieve what you think is 'perfect happy-vibing Witch Queen' status when you are successfully doing your own thing by yourself.

But the rewards are multiplied in a coven. It can also be a lot of fun! A coven can be an amazingly supportive and nurturing environment. However, a coven should never be a substitute for professional therapy. For example, within a structured teaching coven, such as The Circle Coven, sometimes members may not get a soft shoulder to sniffle upon, but a firm reminder to accept responsibility for actions and words.

Study groups

If you can't find the perfect coven, my advice is to stop looking. Instead, attend local events or start a grassroots witchcraft study group. This way, you can meet like-minded people in an informal setting, and talk about topics which interest you all.

The simplest way to go about starting a study group is to decide on a safe, central and accessible space. People will feel more comfortable meeting in a public place, such as a coffee shop or park, rather than in a private venue. Advertise the time and place, and describe your aim for the meeting, for example: "I'd like to form a study group with others interested in witchcraft." Then, on the day, you turn up early, use something to identify your gathering (such as a bright flag or table centrepiece) and you wait. As a general rule, less than a quarter of people who 'like' your online event post will turn up. But those people who do make the effort to turn up will do so because they really want to participate.

> The perfect coven may be the one you create yourself, with other witches you've met at workshops or meetups.

Safety

Unfortunately, there are dodgy people who also happen to be witches or Pagans. There aren't many, but they do exist, and they usually skirt on the fringes of the Pagan community. At times, it's difficult to work out whether someone is just slightly eccentric or if they are potentially dangerous.

While some Australian states have public Pagan support organisations, these vary in effectiveness and approach. I thoroughly recommend the resources provided by the Australian Pagan Awareness Network (PAN), particularly the *Safety in the Circle* brochure:<www.paganawareness.net.au/get-informed/ publications /safety-in-the-circle>

FUNDAMENTALS: Starting Points

This section contains information that should be read before progressing through the rest of the book. Yes, it's tempting to flick straight to the spellwork section, but attempting spells and rituals without having some fundamental knowledge is, at best, ineffective and, at worst, dangerous to the psyche.

Ethics

It's handy to have guidelines and ethics to inform our activities as modern-day witches. Two of the best-known, The Threefold Law and The Wiccan Rede have been around since the 1960s. We partially integrate these into our coven's ethical system. There are two other, more recent 'truisms' which are frequently cited on social media. These are 'intent is everything' and 'do whatever feels right'. Let's look at these one at a time.

The Threefold Law
While The Threefold Law has a specific meaning to Wiccans, other witches completely disregard it or apply it in different ways. Some witches explain The Threefold Law means that anything (such as positive or negative thoughts) you send forth into the universe comes back to you three times stronger. And if someone causes harm to you or your loved ones, that person deserves to receive back three times the amount of harm (or bad luck) in response.

Unfortunately, the otherworlds do not work in such a simple, straightforward manner. If The Threefold Law literally worked like that, we'd all be doing good deeds and reaping the rewards by the barrowload, wouldn't we? However, I believe that it can serve to remind us that for every action, there is some form of consequence.

The Wiccan Rede
'Eight words the Wiccan Rede fulfil: An it harm none, do what ye will.'
(Doreen Valiente, 1964)

Living your life in strict accordance with The Wiccan Rede is impossible to achieve. And how do you define harm? For example, someone makes a deep cut into another person's abdomen with a sharp knife. Surely, that action is causing the ultimate harm! However, this activity brings about healing, rather than harm, when a cancerous growth is removed by a skilled surgeon's scalpel.

Within the coven, we prefer to see the Rede as gentle advice, reminding us of potential consequences arising from deliberately baneful actions. However, not all witches see the Rede in that way. As in the case of The Threefold Law, there is no universal understanding or agreement among witches.

At a fundamental level, when you do harm to others, you could be harming yourself, particularly if this means holding onto toxic, angry emotions. The Rede provides us with a reminder about the interconnectedness of life. But at times, a witch has got to do what a witch has got to do, according to their own guides, gods, higher self or family/community requirements.

Personally, I find it far more useful to modify the Rede to 'Do what thou wilt, and accept that there are consequences for your actions'.

Intent is everything
Myth busted. This is a misguided and erroneous statement. Think about it. Word by word. As there's only three words, it won't take too long.

Intent is not everything. It simply *cannot* be everything. There are a multitude of factors governing the seen and unseen worlds, and focused intent – while absolutely necessary – is only one of these things. Intent is important; crucial, yes. Everything though? Nope. Frequently, actions in the material world are also needed to bring about the required result. For some things, physical action is the most appropriate course to take, rather than spellwork.

Do whatever you feel is right
This oft sprouted 'wisdom' doesn't really float within a magical training group such as a witch coven. Frequently, within our coven, we are called to do things which feel awkward or unsettling. Some activities or rituals are undertaken to deliberately create feelings of unease or discomfort, to create a shift in mindset. So, at that time, or for some time afterwards, it may not feel these are the 'right' things to do, particularly if there is an unconscious association equating 'rightness' with 'comfort zone'.

Taking risks and sailing your boat away from the harbour (metaphorically speaking) can feel quite scary and unsettling. When we take risks, it often doesn't feel right. It may indeed feel very wrong. People can feel a profound sense of terror or anxiety with some changes wrought through spiritual challenges. But witchcraft is about transformation, not about maintaining the status quo. Nature is not stationary. Growth can be painful, and at times we need to deliberately shake free from the constraints that limit us. And if you are not willing to do that because you are avoiding things that might make you feel uncomfortable.... well, there you are, still in the harbour with your pristine un-sailed boat moored aft and fore until it rots away from disuse. What an unsatisfying life.

At other times you simply don't know what feels right, as your emotions are in turmoil, or it's a new and unfamiliar situation. In that case, you must make the best choice you can, based on the information you have, and the outcomes you desire. And take the leap.

Just to be sparklingly crystal-clear, actions which are harmful to life, limb or sanity are never sanctioned at any time within The Circle Coven.

Meditation

'I define magic as the art of causing changes to take place in consciousness in accordance with will...'
Dion Fortune's definition of magic,
<www.dionfortune.co.uk/articles/dion-fortune-quotations>

As meditation involves deliberately changing our consciousness, it is central to magick and therefore to witchcraft. Meditation is arguably the most important practice you can undertake and is the keystone of developing psychic abilities and promoting awareness of the otherworlds. The more often you meditate (effectively), the greater the benefits. Yes, it really is as simple as that.

Meditation:
- facilitates communication with your higher self/the divine
- enables you to shift away from the pressures and stresses of mundane life
- helps to solve problems in a non-logical manner
- assists you to become more patient, relaxed and less anxious
- enables effective magick
- facilitates shadow work
- enhances physical, mental and psychic senses.

My previous High Priestess, Rhianna, believed meditation could provide the answer to pretty much any problem. In response to our queries or tales of woe, she would often adopt a far-off and mystic gaze, and respond with: "Why don't you meditate on it?"

Us, as learner witches: Big sigh and eye roll. (Naturally, we tried our best not to let her see the eye roll.)

However, as a coven leader, I have now found that phrase to be sage advice in response to a new witch with complex questions: "Why don't you meditate on that?"

So, what is meditation? In *Buckland's Complete Book of Witchcraft*, Raymond Buckland calls meditation a:

> '... listening to the Higher Self or, if you prefer, the Inner Self, the Creative Force, the Higher Consciousness; even the gods themselves. It can be all of these.'

There are many ways to enter an altered consciousness or meditative state, including repetitive movements, deep breathing or listening to certain sounds. There are also many forms of meditation, including focused meditation (where all your attention is placed on one focal point, for example, the breath), or open-monitoring meditation. Mindfulness meditation techniques, such as those suggested by Jon Kabbat Zin, are definitely worth exploring for their many benefits.

No-mind meditation is a 'no thought' or classic form of meditation. It aims to help us access the deeper states of consciousness, sometimes known as the still point or the silence within. No-mind status is achieved when the internal monkey mind chatter is temporarily stilled and we experience the realms of the mental, spiritual or Akashic planes.

Accessing deeper levels of consciousness usually requires more discipline and practice than simple creative visualization or guided meditation. I have found the quieter and deeper, silent meditative no-mind state is where the 'real work' happens, and truer guidance and insights are received. So, it's well worth persevering with this technique.

Having said that, there is no 'one size fits all' method of meditation that will suit every person. Try experimenting with different kinds to find the method that suits you best. However, I recommended you try a particular technique a few times before giving up, as it is unlikely that you will achieve immediate results.

When shouldn't you meditate?

The process of turning the mind's focus inward upon itself causes channels to be opened between the conscious and unconscious parts of the mind, which can make us feel very uncomfortable. Our unconscious mind is a storage place for those actions, reactions, words, feelings and experiences we have forgotten or don't frequently access during everyday consciousness. Some of these 'forgotten' experiences are unpleasant or painful. When re-accessed by meditation, they can feel as fresh and raw as when they first occurred. If you have any major concerns about meditation, chat with your healthcare practitioner.

Meditation is the cornerstone of inner work, but here are some situations when it might be better to take a break:

+ If you are severely depressed, meditation can sometimes create a worse emotional state by highlighting or amplifying painful emotions. In this case, consulting with a health care professional is a better option.
+ A 'third eye headache' in the middle of your forehead commonly occurs when people start meditating and doing energy work. Drink lots of water and give meditation a break for a couple of days until your headache settles.
+ Your circumstances change and you are under severe and extreme stress. It can be next to impossible to meditate in this state, so doing deep breathing and body relaxation exercises is more effective.

Elements of a meditation
Crowley, in *Magick, Liber ABA: Book IV*, explains how to meditate very simply:

> '*Sit still.* Stop thinking. *Shut up. Get out!*'

However, most people prefer to have a bit more information, so read on.

In essence, meditation includes the following aspects:
1. Preparation
2. Protection
3. Physical and mental relaxation
4. The meditation or visualisation activity
5. Returning to everyday consciousness

We shall explore these in more detail, one by one.

1. Preparation
Meditating in the same place and at the same time each day makes it easier to meditate effectively. Some of our coven members have a designated meditation chair at home to help them make meditation part of their routine.

In the coven, we do not encourage people to meditate in a lying down position as it is easier to fall asleep and you may condition your mind to only meditate when your body is recumbent, which isn't terribly practical. I recommend that routine meditation is done in either of the following positions, recognizing modifications may be required due to physical limitations:

- Sit cross-legged on the ground or floor. Arms are relaxed by your side, with hands along your legs or in your lap. Keep your hands open (no crossed fingers) or form a circle with your finger and thumb. Keep your back straight.
- Sit on a straight-backed chair. Feet flat on the ground, arms relaxed by your side, hands cupped open or resting on your thighs. Keep your back straight and do not cross your legs or fingers.

Switch off your mobile phone and/or take the home phone off the hook. Make sure you won't be disturbed.

Some people like to play music. This is an individual choice, but be aware the music you play can influence your meditation. Burn incense if you like. Ensure it is safe to leave candles or incense burning unattended (if you use them) and away from the reach of curious animal companions.

Wear loose, comfortable clothing. Preferably, remove your shoes, socks and stockings to reduce constriction and aid 'flow' to the soles of your feet. Ensure you are dressed suitably for the climate. It's not unusual to return to everyday consciousness feeling icy cold after sitting still for an extended time.

Allow yourself enough time; generally, 30 minutes is adequate. If time constraints are an issue, experiment with alarms on your electrical devices to ease you gently out of the meditative state. Short, regular sessions are generally better than irregular, long sessions, or fitting meditation in around your weekend plans. Try to integrate meditation into your routine for best results.

2. Protection

While meditating, you are opening yourself to many subtle changes and, in some ways, you are leaving your body behind. Would you go on holidays and leave your house unlocked? Unlikely. Before you meditate, routinely do some form of protection as good magical housekeeping. Some recommended ways are:

- Define a protective boundary around your body (or at the edges of the room) by tracing a circle using your index finger pointed to the ground.
- Imagine your aura as a non-penetrable shiny white egg around your body.
- Say a prayer or intentional statement of protection, such as: "May the Goddess bless me during my meditation and keep me safe from harm."

If you'd like additional information regarding everyday magical protection, please see the chapters *Grounding, Centering and Protection*, *Everyday Magical Practices* and *Energetic Cleansing*.

3. Relaxation

Without first relaxing your mind and body, it is difficult to enter a deep state of meditation. Here are some simple ways to relax your body:

✦ Focus on your breathing. Pay attention to your diaphragm, which is the area above your belly button. Feel it expanding and contracting as you breathe in and out.

✦ Cyclic breathing is particularly helpful to bring about a relaxed state. Breathe in while counting to four in your mind. Hold your breath while counting to four. Breathe out while counting to four. And relax your diaphragm while counting to four. Then breathe in again for the count of four. You may like to start with a count of two or three, if four is too difficult at first.

✦ Visualise yourself floating like a light feather or a fluffy cloud, feeling all tension leaving your body as you drift gently along.

✦ Starting at your feet and working upwards to finish at your head, tense then relax each body part. After you release the tension, visualise that body part filled with white light.

There are good reasons why people find it difficult to meditate effectively. Meditation is a special kind of concentration, which withdraws the energy (physical, mental, emotional) we usually expend on multiple external factors, and turns it inward to examine a single, predetermined concept. This is hard work for our lazy minds, which aren't used to functioning in that way.

Mental relaxation is usually the hardest aspect. This is because all the humdrum thoughts of the day interrupt us, and our mind does its best to distract us from the job at hand by throwing fascinating information into our consciousness. Often when people start meditating, they are *more* aware of their thoughts. This is normal, as often we run on autopilot, unaware of the inner thoughts directing our lives. Meditation helps us become aware of our usual monkey mind talk, so we can access those quieter, chatter-free spaces.

Accept that the first few moments of meditation will likely involve some inner chatter. After a short time, release those thoughts and let them go. Don't remain fixated on silly, seductive yabber. Sometimes it can take weeks to get past that internal blabber stage, so don't be too quick to give up hope.

Persevere with your fledgling meditation practice.

There are also often physical distractions which occur when trying to meditate. It is incredible how itchy your nose (or ear, or hand) can suddenly become when you sit down with the intention of meditating. And noises! Suddenly you are aware of a dog barking three blocks away. Once again, sit there and let these distractions fade away as you ease into a meditative state.

4. Meditation and visualisation

Guided meditations are a great way to build your practice. There are many freely available on the internet, or you can pre-record your own using a script then play it back to yourself. Visualisation during meditation involves 'seeing' pictures or images in your mind's eye that are not present in your current physical surroundings. Sensations while in a state of altered consciousness can include sounds, smells and tactile sensations (touch).

Some people find visualisation very easy to do, but for others it takes time and effort to acquire the ability to clearly see or imagine yourself as part of an inner landscape. Unless you have a condition called antaphasia (where you can't 'see' any internal images), here are some simple exercises to help improve your visualisation process.

Put a simple item such as an apple or pencil in front of you. Now try to recreate that image in your mind's eye. From time to time, open your eyes and check for accuracy. Visualising a candle is always a nice exercise. When you are confident at being able to hold a simple image in your mind's eye, next try rotating the image to 'see' it from different angles. When you are successful at manipulating simple images, move onto complex images. Try to see a whole room, or the front of your house. Finally, practice visualising images with your physical eyes open but unfocused, but I suggest don't do that while driving.

5. Returning to everyday consciousness

Failure to 'close down' after a meditation can leave you vague, fuzzy headed and tired. It can also leave you open to attracting disturbances in your energetic field. It is important to have a clear and defined transition between altered consciousness and everyday consciousness states. Techniques to do this include:

+ If you are following a guided meditation, retrace your path to the starting point where you entered the inner landscape.
+ Pay attention to how you feel as you exit the meditation. This may feel like a rushing or sinking sensation, or an increasing awareness of your

physical surroundings. Don't stand up until you are confident that you are 'back' in normal consciousness.
- ✦ Stretch your body and wriggle your toes and fingers.
- ✦ If required, stamp your feet or clap your hands. State firmly, "I demand to return to this place and time."
- ✦ Drink lots of water and have something yummy to eat.

The Inner Planes

When we go on a trip to an unfamiliar place, we follow a map or guide to gain an understanding of the terrain and route. The otherworlds we visit during meditation also have terrain to navigate so it's just as handy to have a map there. Each of the inner planes in the otherworlds is associated with different experiences, symbolism, colours, entrance ways and entry keys. While that seems quite precise, the subtle spaces of the inner planes are not measurable by any quantifiable scientific methodology.

A simplistic way to understand the landscape of the inner planes is to imagine them as a layered cake. The cake rests on a plate, which represents the lowest, or most materially dense plane, i.e. the physical plane. Each layer, divided by cream, has different ingredients, initially quite dense but becoming lighter with each layer. The bottom layer is chocolate mud cake, the next is fruit cake, followed by cinnamon tea cake which is crowned by a light, airy sponge layer. At the top of this most unusual cake, there is a whole lot of whipped, frothy stuff, which relates to the most subtle/highest plane, i.e. the spiritual plane.

My apologies to the purists who might be horrified at this cake analogy.

Knowledge of the inner planes assists us to better understand the magical notions of 'thoughts are things' and 'as above, so below'. There's an occult principle which suggests every event which occurs on the physical plane has previously occurred on the less dense or higher planes. For these reasons, a working knowledge of the inner planes is valuable.

The system the coven uses is adapted from Theosophy and the works of Dion Fortune. Here's a brief outline of the inner planes or dimensions, according to that system.

Physical plane
This plane is the place of material and physical matters. It includes objects that are observed, measured and felt with our five senses. The physical plane is the densest plane of manifestation.

Etheric plane

This dimension includes less concrete or dense forms of energy in comparison to the physical plane, and it overlaps into the astral realms. Etheric substances may be observed when observing the auric/energy field around people, trees, animals and other items. Some tips about how to do this are provided in the *Energy sensing, Auras and Chakras* chapter. The etheric plane links to personal and physical wellbeing.

Astral planes

Emotions, such as anger, sorrow, or joy are keys to the astral domains. Much of what exists on the lower astral is temporary, fluid and impermanent, and it is named the 'plane of illusion' for good reason. The astral plane is also the realm where entities, spirit beings, and ghosts may interact with us. This dimension is easily accessed via altered states of consciousness; all we have to do is daydream and we are in the astral.

Mental planes

The mental planes are associated with thoughts and abstract concepts rather than emotions. Thought forms (energetic patterns or beings) are created on this level. Unlike the astral, the beings and places of the mental planes have a longer 'life' and permanence.

Spiritual planes

These are the most subtle, remote and intangible planes, and therefore more difficult to access deliberately. Some esoteric traditions believe you must cross a metaphysical chasm (the 'abyss') to access the spiritual planes. The spiritual planes are the dwelling places of deity, the Higher Self and the Akashic records.

Spirit Guides

Many witches interact with spirit guides or allies. There is no 'one size fits all' when it comes to describing spirit guides, as perceptions vary widely. Some people believe they have a series of guides interacting with them across their life, changing according to personal need and spiritual growth. Other people believe their spirit guide is a facet of their own higher self or Holy Guardian Angel. Spirit guides may take the appearance of people, animals, aliens or wisps of smoke, but rarely appear in a material, physical body. Regardless of their form, spirit guides are positive presences who look out for you and offer good guidance or advice.

I am not going to tell you what your spirit guide is – or is not – with one notable exception. Although some spirit guides have trickster traits, they will rarely give you consistently nasty, critical or mean messages. Spirit guides do not speak like your judgemental mother or your nagging father or a cruel friend who tells you that you are stupid or dumb or worthless. If you are receiving this sort of message, it isn't your spirit guide chatting with you; it's your 'inner critic' or 'monkey mind'. Sometimes you might feel like your spirit guide gives the occasional eye roll or feels exasperated at how you are refusing to listen to (their) good advice. But that feels quite different to being harassed or harangued by unpleasant voices inside your head, which is not the role of a spirit guide.

Meeting your spirit guide
If you aren't already in touch with your spirit guide/s, it is possible to meet them through guided meditation or dream incubation. Set a clear intention of what you want to achieve. You may like to say, "During this meditation, I will meet my guide/s" or "Over the next three nights while dreaming, I ask that my spirit guide/s are revealed to me."

- Say aloud your intentions, three times. Because three is a magical number.
- Completely relax your body and enter a meditative state.
- Visualise yourself in a location where you would like to meet your guide/s. Choose an inner landscape with personal meaning for you. Perhaps a

- beach, a forest grove, or an ancient temple. It's completely up to you.
- When you are in the 'right place and space', ask clearly and respectfully that your guide appears.
- Now, wait. Look at what is around you. Potentially, you could be beckoned to journey to another meeting place.
- Remember that your guide/s or allies may or may not appear in a human shape.
- When you do meet your guide/s you might feel a profound sense of belonging, joy, love, connection or relief.
- If something presents as your 'guide' but is unpleasant, condemning or abusive towards you, state firmly "Leave me alone", and see them withdrawing from you. This being is not your guide but is likely to be an unhelpful entity or, potentially, an aspect of your shadow self. Guides or allies can have a peculiar sense of humour, but that's quite different from being nasty. At any stage, if you feel unsafe, stop the meditation, and repeat it again at another time, ensuring there is a circle of protection around you and you are in a good emotional state.
- When you do meet your guide/s, ask for their name, as this is a powerful link to them. Carefully note their appearance and clothing. Are they carrying anything? Do they offer you a gift? Also, ask them how you can find and connect with them again.
- At the conclusion of your meeting, and before leaving, thank them.
- Return to normal consciousness and scrupulously document what you saw and experienced during your meditation.

Energy Sensing, Auras and Chakras

Every physical thing consists of energy. Objects we perceive as being solid, such as chairs and tables, are made up of particles, vibrating at different frequencies. This is a basic principle of science, as well as being an important occult principle. Our bodies are not simply bones, blood and flesh; they also integrate energetic systems. Physical and energetic bodies sustain and complement each other in complex synergy. Through our bodies circulates the 'life force'; you may have heard it called qi (Mandarin language) or prana (Sanskrit language). Incidentally, both these words are associated with the breath, or air.

The energetic system which extends beyond the physical body is called the aura. The aura usually exists in a state of flux and change, as auras don't have consistently defined boundaries. Within the physical body, we have energy centres which link to places in the body, as well as channels between these energy centres. These channels of subtle energy are called meridians in Traditional Chinese Medicine, or nadis in Sanskrit. In addition to the energetic centres associated with body organs, living beings have the subtle energy centres which are commonly called chakras.

Chakras are energy vortexes which connect us to universal energy, allowing us to absorb energy to revitalise and also to share or direct energy. The word chakra (which means wheel or circle in Sanskrit) and associated concepts have been adopted from Indian traditions. Due to the influence of mystics and magicians in the Victorian era, learning about chakra systems is often a hallmark of contemporary witchery. If there was ever a European map of the non-physical body similar to the chakra system, it is no longer available.

Most of the time, people are not aware of the energy flows through and around their body. They may only notice when sudden changes in emotion or illness significantly impact their energy levels. Strong passions or focused activities can open up energy centres or, alternatively, minimise or block the flow of vitality.

Though there are many energy-centre systems in use, The Circle Coven prefers to use a seven-chakra system which links to the colours of a rainbow.

The chakras are seen as shining, changeable structures of energy at specific points of the body. The crown and the base chakras are visualised at either end of the seven chakras. These end chakras are linked by a major, central energy channel, that connects with the other five chakras. Occasionally, we add in the energy centres on the palms of our hands and the soles of our feet, as those chakras can help us to direct energy and connect us to the Earth.

Auras and energy sensing

With practice, you can see the aura surrounding the body of a living being, particularly the etheric body, which is the densest layer of the aura. The best way to do this is to ask a friend to sit in front of a dark-coloured wall, in dim lighting. Don't look directly at their body or face. Focus your eyes to look at the space beyond their body, above their shoulders, or to the side of their head.

As your perception develops, you may begin to see a pale grey-glowing shimmer radiating beyond the physical body. This is the etheric field, and is relatively easy to see, unless you are in bright sunlight. Another way to learn to see the etheric field is to look at the space around your own hands when you are in a dim environment. No, it's not your imagination. You are seeing the glowing edges of the etheric field.

People 'see' auras differently. There is no correct or consistent way to see the colours in an aura, but it does usually involve the psychic senses rather than your physical eyes. An auric field will often appear as an 'overlay' to the material item. Maybe you might see flashes of light, or shifting colours, or a semi-transparent bubble around a living being. Remember, humans are not the only ones with auras. Practice, experiment, and work out the associations between what you 'see' and what is occurring for that person.

Here's a table with the key points about the chakra system used in the coven.

Chakra	Function	Location	Colour	Correspondences
Base	Sex and survival, life	Base of spine	Red	Element: Earth Associations: Physical plane, our bodies, grounding, security, structure, manifestation, stability. Astrological planet: Saturn Connect: Movement of any kind, consciously eat food, expel waste products.

Sacral plexus	Energy, strength and fluidity	Lower abdomen	Orange	Element: Water Associations: Instincts, sexuality, feelings, fluidity, creativity, sensuality. Astrological planet: Jupiter Connect: Swim, dance, be creative or make something.
Solar plexus	Power, will and self-esteem	Navel	Yellow	Element: Fire Associations: Ego, authority, health, vitality, determination, decision making, confidence. Astrological planet: Mars Connect: Be competitive, leadership roles, spend time in sunlight.
Heart	Emotions, love and healing	Mid-chest	Green	Element: Water Associations: Compassion, connection, generosity, integration. Astrological planet: Venus Connect: Focus on self-love, love of and for others, healing.
Throat	Communication and expression	Throat	Blue	Element: Air Associations: Communication, expression of emotions, integrity, self. Astrological planet: Mercury Connect: Sing, chant, make speeches, release frustrations.
Third eye	Intuition and psychic ability	Brow	Indigo	Element: Fire Associations: Divination, inner sight, wisdom, knowing. Astrological planet: Moon Connect: Meditate, keep a journal, practice divination.
Crown	The divine and spirituality	Top of head	Violet	Element: Spirit Associations: The Universe, pure consciousness, Grace, connection, awareness, bliss. Astrological planet: Sun Connect: Meditate, reflect, focus on spirituality.

Opening and closing the chakras

Just as your lungs automatically breathe air in and out of your physical body, your chakras regulate the flow of energies into and out of your body's energy system. Here's an exercise to help you become proficient in opening and closing your chakras.

1. Sit in a comfortable, straight-backed chair. Let your mind go blank.
2. Focus your attention on your base chakra. Imagine your base chakra opening like a flower bud spreading its petals. See the colour pulsating and vibrant. Alternatively, see each chakra as initially being a tiny ball of coloured light, and then expand it out to basketball size, before visualising it shrinking to the size of a small apple.
3. When the chakra has grown as large as feels comfortable, imagine it slowly closing, until it is small and steady. You can also imagine it completely closed if you wish.
4. Repeat this for all chakras.
5. Come out of your meditative state and ground yourself by eating or drinking.

Cleansing the chakras

Just like other parts of the body, chakras can feel sluggish or blocked, particularly if you've had prolonged stress or ill health. The following exercise is a nifty way to cleanse your chakras. It's light-hearted, yet very effective.

1. Start at the crown chakra and work down.
2. Imagine you are standing inside the crown chakra, as if you had shrunk to be a tiny person. See yourself inside the ball-like chakra, like it is a blown-up, glowing balloon. You have a hose with a powerful jet of water (don't worry about where the hose is connected to – it's magick!), some strong detergent and a scrubbing brush.
3. Visualise the walls of the chakra as looking murky and dirty. Because of the muck on the walls, the light is dim and the colour is dull.
4. Get to work, scrubbing and hosing the inside walls of the chakra, as if you were cleaning dirty windows. As you clean, see the colour become brighter and clearer.
5. At the bottom of each chakra, there's a magick drain hole. Through it, all the gunk flows downwards and out into the universe for composting.
6. Continue downwards through each chakra, until you visualise them all as being shiny and clean.

Grounding, Centering, and Protection

Grounding, centering and protection are three words which are mentioned frequently in witchy circles, but often given different meanings. At core, they relate to energy work, so let's consider each one carefully and explore some techniques.

Centering

Centering involves psychically steadying yourself and becoming energetically calm and focused. Ideally, do this before each spellwork session, meditation or ritual. Centering is also a useful standalone technique to calm or soothe you during hectic or tense times, such as a bad day at work or a fraught dinner with family. Here are some simple techniques:

✦ The quickest and easiest method to centre yourself is to focus on your breathing. Let your diaphragm rise and fall with each breath you take. Be aware of your body. Relax and release any tensions or strong emotions with each breath. When you feel a sense of peace and poise, you are becoming centered.

✦ Stand upright and imagine there is a string attached to the top of your head, and another attached to the bottom of your feet. Feel your body stretch gently upwards and downwards at the same time with your posture becoming still, straight and balanced.

✦ Chant a word such as 'Aum' (or 'Om'). Get a good vibrational feeling happening through your body.

✦ Visualise yourself as a tree, with roots emerging from your feet (or your base chakra) sinking deeply into the ground. Lift your arms, or visualise branches growing out of your head/fingertips, reaching up to the sky. Your spine and body are a solid trunk, connected between earth and sky.

✦ Open each of your chakras as described in the previous chapter.

Grounding

Sometimes people refer to grounding as being the first stage of energy work, but within the coven, we consider grounding to be the final stage to complete a magical activity. Grounding is where you 'shut down' or 'shut off' from energy work and return and connect to everyday consciousness. Effective grounding will prevent spacey feelings and disconnection between mind and body.

The simplest and fastest way to ground is to eat something, as food activates the physical process of digestion and brings you back to the mundane world. Avoid foods which have stimulating effects; proteins and complex carbohydrates are better choices. Drinking fluids also helps to ground. Here are some other techniques to try:

- Place the palms of your hands on the ground. Take deep breaths in and out. Feel the excess energy leave you and flow into the earth where it is transformed and grounded.
- Hug a tree. Let the additional energy seep away.
- Hug a consenting person.
- Have a really good stretch.
- Shake your body and do a little dance. Flick off excess energy like invisible drops of water.
- Meaningfully saying, aloud or internally: "I am now grounded and safe."

Personal protection and shielding

Shielding describes the process of creating and maintaining magical personal protection. There are many ways to shield or protect yourself, from a simple visualisation right through to a complex ritual. Usually, simple approaches are effective. You can:

- Wear a talisman, amulet, pentagram pendant or piece of magically consecrated jewellery.
- Complete a 'I'm surrounded by an impervious white bubble' visualisation.
- Wear clothing that has magical significance, due to colour or design, such as a shawl.
- Trace a circle around yourself using your finger and visualise your aura safely within it.
- Imagine you are inside an egg-shaped mirror ball with the outer surfaces reflecting back unwanted energies.
- Try to be true in word and deed, which negates a lot – but not all – negativity.

Reincarnation

Many years ago, my science teacher told me religion was invented to explain the three big questions: how we got here, why we are here, and where we go when we die. It was an unsatisfying answer, which failed to offer a decent explanation to my enquiring teenage mind. Is there really nothing before birth, followed by a purposeless life of survival, procreation and reproduction, ending in complete extinguishment of the soul?

By the way, the words spirit or soul can mean different things, but here I'm using the word 'soul' as the perpetual, individual/personal and continuous entity or spark of life.

Orthodox Christianity tells us that the souls of dead people are either transported to Heaven or Hell. The souls of the pious go up to the place of happiness, and the naughty ones experience eternal suffering down below. Even though you may not be Christian, this religion has had a massive influence on Western culture. However, it doesn't seem to provide a terribly convincing explanation for where our souls come from before being encapsulated into our bodies.

Witches, on the other hand, aren't locked into rigid belief systems of Heaven, Hell or even the idea that we have only one life on Earth. Reincarnation gives a satisfying alternative, as it suggests that the soul begins a new life in a new physical form after the death of the body. Concepts of reincarnation are included in some contemporary religions, as well as being part of historical belief systems. The mystery schools of Eleusis in ancient Greece taught about the immortal soul and the spiral ascent of destiny. Unlike a candle flame which is gone after being quenched, it just seems to make sense that our souls, which breathe life into our physical bodies, have an ongoing existence before birth and after death.

Many people can share stories of experiences relating to other times in history, or being aware of other lifetimes not associated with their current physical body or situations. People who have experienced physical death and then been brought back to life hint there is more than one existence. Sensations of deja vu associated with people and places that seem irrational or out of time and place also suggest we experience more than one life.

The seasonal cycle of the Wheel of the Year reminds us that without death there can be no rebirth and without rebirth there is no ongoing life. When you die, it is only the passing of the physical body, not the permanent death of the soul. The soul goes on to a new life with new lessons each time. Many Pagans believe there is a resting place in between lives, sometimes called the Summerlands. It's also believed we choose when, where, and to whom we are born, taking into account the soul's lessons, previous actions and former relationships. This concept though is quite tricky, as it seems to blame people for circumstances which appear outside of their control in this lifetime. Nevertheless, for others, this is a satisfying and meaningful explanation.

Many people have the experience of meeting someone for the first time, yet feeling the overwhelming sense you have met that person before. Sometimes this feeling of familiarity will be accompanied by a sense of attraction, or repulsion. It seems that our soul recognises another soul from a previous life (or lives), even though each person now has a different body in new circumstances.

One explanation is that we all first come into existence with many others at the same time. These beings are known as your soul group. A soul group will usually travel with you throughout the continuity of time and be around you in some form. You will feel safest and most comfortable when you are with them. Each person in your soul group will have things to teach you about your lives, important or small. These souls are like a family and in between each life you will try to meet up with some of them at various times on the higher plane and on Earth. Strong love, or hate, also can create bonds lasting across lifetimes.

It's convenient to consider our soul journeys as occurring in a line, going from past into the present and onwards into the nebulous future. This sequential model helps us to keep track of time and our place in it. However, there are other theories which suggest that we are living a multitude of lives simultaneously, or in many dimensions all at the same time. These are concepts to reflect on when pondering reincarnation.

The most important life is the one you are living right now.

Coming Out of the Broom Closet

Some new witches feel an overwhelming urge to let everyone – particularly those people nearest and dearest to them – know they have embraced a new form of spirituality. This might be an act of defiance or rebellion, metaphorically sticking up the middle finger and publicly rejecting old patterns of behaviour or social conditioning. Calling oneself a witch can have fantastic shock value and be quite liberating in the right setting. Other times, people wish to share the news of their witchery because it's been such an overwhelmingly positive experience, and why shouldn't people know about it? In this case, there is a genuine need to explain, share and discuss their new knowledge or attitudes with friends and family.

I would like to suggest a middle ground between declaring to all and sundry that "I am a witch! A follower of the old ways!" or secretly spitting out your communion wafer. Ask yourself: does every single person in my life – personal, work, family, friends – need to know I am a witch? Perhaps there are some people you feel comfortable telling, but in other settings (for example, paid employment) it is not appropriate to discuss matters of alternative spirituality.

Some Circle Coven members (including myself) have decided not to discuss our path with work colleagues or clients, due to job security concerns. This approach leads us to be quite imaginative when explaining 'what I did last night', while leaving out the W word. Some strategies members have successfully used include referring to a meditation group, a women's healing circle, a (mysterious) 'ladies group', or medieval society, which is incidentally a perfect way to justify the smell of wood smoke in hair. I've let my close work-mates know I read Tarot cards, but apart from having a few intriguing rocks on my office desk, that's as far as it goes for my disclosure.

When telling others about your newly embraced witcheries, it's important to be aware they may react in a negative manner, according to their own values. This is more likely to occur if your disclosure comes as a complete surprise to them, or if it is an affront to strong religious beliefs. There could be long-term consequences for your relationship, which might never be amicably resolved. In some cases, of course, that is a necessary thing. Sometimes we need to have the space and freedom to grow in a manner that is meaningful and positive for us. This can mean reducing contact with people who bring overwhelming stress, control or drama.

It is never OK to 'out' someone. Never.

Although witchcraft is legal in many Westernised countries, this doesn't equate to an accurate understanding of modern witchcraft. Instead of a thought-bubble linking witchcraft with love of nature or a desire to learn about the mysteries of life, there can be an automatic association of witchcraft with evil. The 'all witches are animal sacrificing Satanists' portrayal certainly adds another layer of complexity to the 'hi Mum, I'm a witch' discussions. It might be handy to get that out of the way early in the conversation. Some forms of Satanism *are* a legitimate spiritual pathway, rather than the hysterical Christian portrayal, but that's a topic for another day.

Some suggestions to manage coming out of the broom closet
- ✦ Spend time deciding who you are going to tell, how you are going to tell them, and when you are going to tell them.
  - *"I've been doing some reading on modern day witches. Did you know they aren't evil? Modern witches try to work in harmony with the Earth. It's something I'm planning to learn more about. Here's a really cool website."*
  - *"I'm not a Christian. I'm a Pagan."*
  - *"I follow an alternative spirituality path. It's called witchcraft."*
  - *"I'm a witch. I believe there is more to life than what we can see or touch."*
- ✦ Provide written information or a website reference.
- ✦ Accept that some people will act in a negative manner initially when you let them know you are a witch. This could be because they care for your welfare and worry about your mental and physical wellbeing.
- ✦ Prepare to defend against pop-culture stereotypes such as hags, warts, or Potterisms.
- ✦ Hope for the best, prepare for the worst, and don't engage in altercations. Walk away and try again later when emotions have calmed down.

FOUNDATIONS: Build Your Practice

It's best to start with a strong foundation before reaching towards the moon and stars. This section includes many essential building blocks to ground, solidify and intensify your witchery practices.

Book of Shadows

A Book of Shadows (BoS) is a book, usually with a black cover, containing information about magical practices. Historically, it's likely to have originated from the keeping of grimoires, books of magic which included instructions about spells, talismans, amulets, astrology, divination, and how to connect with entities. Grimoires were used by ceremonial magicians and cunning folk in Europe and England. The Book of Abramelin and The Key of Solomon are two famous grimoires.

More recently, tradition dictated one BoS existed in a Wiccan-style coven, and this was kept by the High Priestess or High Priest. Novice witches copied the relevant sections of the BoS by hand into their own BoS, which was a laborious and slow task. As they advanced, they were able to copy extra information from the coven BoS into their own.

In some traditions, if/when a covener left the coven (or died), their transcribed BoS was burnt. The burning of a BoS has less meaning today, as it's easy to photograph or electronically scan the pages of a handwritten BoS.

BoS – The Circle Coven style

We have a Circle Coven BoS, which has a red leather cover, smattered in wax from rituals over the years. Our BoS contains handwritten Initiation rituals, oaths, and a year-by-year record of Coven activities, including membership. This book also contains the lineage of The Circle Coven and is not for general viewing.

Our everyday rituals, lessons and practices are stored electronically. For rituals, we print out the specific file and insert the pages into a display folder, which is placed on the altar. This is a practical and all-weather solution (and also protects the pages from bat poo).

Within the coven, we encourage members to create their own personal and handwritten BoS, as this is a satisfying and rewarding activity. There are no hard and fast rules about what to include in your BoS as the content is completely up to you. Suggestions include rituals; herbal, crystal and healing lore; incantations and chants; spells and divination methods; beautiful or meaningful artwork.

I also strongly recommend keeping a magical diary of experiences relating to rituals and spells in a separate book or diary kept just for this purpose. Over months and years, it's easy to lose track of what you did, when you did it and why, so consistent journaling is a valuable trait. At the end of each year, I create a summary of key activities in an electronic document, which helps me compare activities across years and decades. It's fascinating to see how some events seem to happen at the same time each year.

Your Personal Altar

Altars have many purposes for witches. They can provide a focal point, or simply be a practical place to put spellwork items. There are no strict rules about what to put on your personal altar (or altars) except to ensure it is firesafe if you light candles or incense. Some people keep the same items on display (that would be me) and others swap things around depending on the season or whim. Your altar can be as minimalist or crowded as you wish, depending on the purpose and your requirements. Some witches will only create an altar when required, keeping their tools out of sight unless they are being used. This also prevents others from touching consecrated ritual items.

If you have small humans or inquisitive animals, locate your altar (or tools) in a drawer or high on a shelf to keep things safe. Or you may prefer to upcycle an old cupboard to display your lovely things in their fullest glory.

In this age of social media, many people share photos of their personal altars. The Circle Coven is 'old school' and we don't encourage this. If you create an altar with the sole intention to impress others, some magical meaning could be diluted. Your special place becomes a focus of your personality, rather than a space where you commune with the Universe and undertake serious spellwork. Keeping silent is an efficient way to keep energies exactly where you intend them to be.

The other reason for this harkens to magical hygiene. Sharing pictures of a personal and permanent working altar creates a nexus, or connection point for other beings – including human beings. In some ways, it's similar to posting your bank account password in a public space. Of course, if you've created a temporary tableau this can be different, and you could then deliberately share that image to amplify your spellwork.

Here are some suggestions about what to include on your personal altar:
- ✦ An altar cloth, which you may like to change for each seasonal celebration or current magical focus
- ✦ Candles or oil burner
- ✦ Representations of deity, such as statues and images

- Your four elemental tools: athame, wand, chalice (or cauldron) and pentacle (see *The Witch's Tools* chapter)
- Incense or charcoal burner
- Bowls for oil, salt and/or water
- Natural objects or special items such as feathers, rocks, shells or photographs.

Correspondences, Elements and Elementals

'It is the knowledge of the method of manipulating these – the elemental essences of each kingdom – which is the basis of practical magic.'
Dion Fortune, The Cosmic Doctrine (page 126).

In magick, the links or shared affinities between objects, concepts, and phenomenon are called correspondences. There are hundreds of systems of correspondences available. This chapter includes those most frequently used by The Circle Coven.

Witches often 'call the quarters' and 'farewell the quarters' as standard parts of sabbat or esbat rituals. The quarters link to the four cardinal directions of East, South, West and North. The quarters are also associated with their own set of correspondences relating to the kingdoms (or realms) of the elements of Air, Fire, Water or Earth. In this context, the elements are based on a historical system rather than the periodic table of elements of modern science.

Each of the four realms has a hierarchical structure with a leader (often called the king, guardian or ruler). Their kingdoms are populated by beings called elementals. The best-known elemental beings and their corresponding kingdom are:

✦ Gnomes, which are most at home in the Earth kingdom
✦ Sylphs associated with the kingdom of Air
✦ Salamanders are the creatures of Fire
✦ Undines are Water kingdom beings.

Quarter correspondences vary between magical traditions, northern and southern hemispheres, and across Australia, with differing rationales for each system. I suggest it is a waste of energy to get into fights over who is right or wrong when assigning directional correspondences.

Instead, it is better to seek to understand the rationale of why something is done a particular way. Some people will simply say they do what they do because it feels right. Although that may seem like a valid response from a solo practitioner, witchcraft is about conscious thought as well as intuition, so it's worth digging deeper into the reasons for your personal practice.

If you work with a coven or participate in a group ritual, it's a good idea for all participants to agree on what is being called, which magical beings you are inviting, and from which direction, for the duration of the ritual. Ceremonies can be unintentionally chaotic unless there is a shared understanding and agreement of ritual practice. That is why our coven endorses a particular system and sticks to it in our rituals.

It might come as a surprise to learn within The Circle Coven, the kingdom of Earth is associated with North, Air with East, Fire with South and Water is linked with West. Spirit is the fifth element and belongs in the centre of the circle. These directional/elemental associations are not common practice in Australia. In fact, our coven follows the conventions of the northern hemisphere when creating a ritual space.

Rather than casting our circle in a sunwise direction (anticlockwise in the southern hemisphere), we cast our circle in a clockwise direction, or deosil (deasil). This word is associated with going in a right direction or moving around an item with the right hand held towards it. Our quarter system also follows northern hemisphere traditions.

Irrespective of where you go upon the Earth, the directions of North, South, East and West remain constant on a map. One doesn't suddenly refer to north as south because you are below the equator. And as each of these cardinal directions has a wealth of associated cultural myths and stories, it seems disrespectful to ignore this lore and, for example, move Boreas, God of the North Wind, to the South.

Another way of looking at things is to imagine that all dimensions, elements and elemental kingdoms are contained within you. That's why I don't get too caught up in worrying about 'correct' southern hemisphere directional correspondences. People have different perceptions, and that's what makes life interesting.

On the next few pages are the cheat sheets for the elemental correspondences most frequently used in The Circle Coven. Many Australian witches prefer to switch North and South correspondences and cast their circle in an anti-clockwise direction, so adjust the correspondences according to your location and preferences.

The Element of Air

Magical tool	Athame or sword
Direction	East
Colour	Yellow
Signs of the zodiac	Gemini, Libra, Aquarius
Magical phrase	Scire – to know
Season	Spring
Hour	Dawn
Elemental kingdom	Sylphs
Elemental ruler	Paralda
Nature	Sky, wind, clouds
Body part	Brain and lungs
Associations	Intellect, thought, inspiration, logic, reasoning and consciousness. Masculine. Dry, expansive and active.
Tarot suit	Swords
Kerub	Eagle
Senses	Hearing and smell
Moon phase	Waxing
Goddess archetype	Maiden
Positive qualities	Dynamic, communicative, intelligent, objective
Unbalanced expression	Vague, forgetful, gossipy, selfish, untruthful, over-intellectualises or over thinks things.
Types of magick	Study, acquiring new knowledge, travel, finding lost items, revealing untruths, bringing freedom.

The Element of Fire

Magical tool	Wand
Direction	South
Colour	Red
Signs of the zodiac	Aries, Leo, Sagittarius
Magical phrase	Velle – to will
Season	Summer
Hour	Noon
Elemental	Salamanders
Elemental ruler	Djinn
Nature	Fire, sun, stars, volcanos
Body part	Head or heart
Associations	Will, change and passion. Masculine. Hot, dry, transformative.
Tarot suit	Wands
Kerub	Lion
Senses	Sight
Moon phase	Full
Goddess archetype	Mother
Positive qualities	Energetic, daring, enthusiastic.
Unbalanced expression	Impatient, aggressive, dominating, egotistical.
Types of magick	Transformation, burning down old structures, destruction, clearing the way for change.

The Element of Water

Magical tool	Chalice, cup or cauldron
Direction	West
Colour	Blue
Signs of the zodiac	Cancer, Scorpio, Pisces
Magical phrase	Audere – to dare
Season	Autumn
Hour	Twilight
Elemental	Undines
Elemental ruler	Niksa
Nature	Water – rivers, streams, oceans, puddles, fog, rain
Body part	Stomach, heart
Associations	Emotions, unconscious mind, empathy. Relationships, connective, collective. Feminine.
Tarot suit	Cups
Kerub	Fish / man
Senses	Taste
Moon phase	Waning
Goddess archetype	Crone
Positive qualities	Sensitive, loving, compassionate, forgiving and flexible.
Unbalanced expression	Irrational, insecure, hypersensitive, perpetual victim.
Types of magick	Happiness, friendship, relationships, fertility, healing, dreaming, psychic arts, purification.

The Element of Earth

Magical tool	Pentacle
Direction	North
Colour	Green
Signs of the zodiac	Taurus, Virgo, Capricorn
Magical phrase	Tacere – to keep silent
Season	Winter
Hour	Midnight
Elemental	Gnomes
Elemental ruler	Ghob
Nature	Rocks, stones, mountains, caves, fields
Body part	Bones, sex organs, flesh
Associations	Feminine. Nurturing, fertile, cold. Sensual, grounded, abundant.
Tarot suit	Pentacles
Kerub	Bull
Senses	Touch
Moon phase	New or dark
Goddess archetype	The Silent One
Positive qualities	Practical, reliable, punctual, steadfast
Unbalanced expression	Materialistic, possessive, superficial, close-minded, inflexible.
Types of magick	Business, money, material wealth, employment, boundaries, prosperity, stability and fertility.

Elemental correspondences together form a system – a network formed by connections.

The Witch's Tools

Tools provide a physical focus for your intentions; some tools are also energy storage reservoirs. There are different schools of thought about whether your tools should be used for mundane acts (such as chopping up the chicken after a ritual) or only used for a specific non-physical, ritual purpose. Our coven practice is that elemental tools are for ritual use only once they have been psychically cleansed and consecrated. For example, the athame is not used to cut any tangible item, as it relates to Air rather than matter.

There are four elemental tools:
+ Athame (pronounced *ath*-a-may, not a-*thay*-may)
+ Wand
+ Pentacle
+ Chalice.

As well as being tools, these items are magical weapons. Therefore, they need to be robust and fit for purpose, rather than flimsy and poorly made. Just to be super clear, the elemental tools are not weapons to cause physical harm or attack people. They are metaphysical weapons, used with skill and authority.

> Never forget that you are the magic, not your tools.

Acquiring your elemental tools
Many witches believe that making your own tools is the most magically powerful way to acquire them, however often this is not possible or practical. Most witches purchase their tools or receive them as gifts. You can then mindfully add embellishments or designs to your tools by painting or carving.

Please be aware expensive does not mean better. In choosing an elemental tool, wait until you find one that sings to you, and try not to haggle over the price as this may imbue your tool with negative energies through unpleasant memories.

Once you have acquired your tools, spend time with them, meditate on them, and learn their purpose and associated mythos.

Do not touch another magical practitioner's tools without their explicit and willing verbal agreement.

Athame

Within The Circle Coven, the athame is the most frequently used elemental tool. The athame is a black-handled knife with a double-sided metal blade. The two sides of the blade are symbolic of the double-edged aspect of power; it cuts both ways. The athame should be at least 15 cm in length to allow a comfortable grasp of the handle. When acquiring an athame, it's essential to also select a suitable sheath so that the athame can be securely worn.

The athame represents the element of Air and the direction of East. It is used to direct energy raised during rituals or spell workings and to banish negativity. The athame is sharp, but not so sharp that it causes harm to its owner or others. As with all magical tools, the athame becomes charged with our touch and usage. Uses include:

- Casting the circle
- Forming a pentagram at each quarter during a ritual
- Consecrating food and offerings
- Cutting non-physical things, such as bonds between people.

If you do wish to cut physical items, a boline (white handled, sharp-bladed knife) can be used for marking objects or chopping things, rather than the athame.

Wand

The wand represents the element of Fire and the direction of South. The wand is used to invoke and to call upon the spirits of Fire. Your wand can be crafted with a male (solar) and female (lunar) ends by adding crystals or carvings, so you can hold either way round according to the emphasis required.

I prefer a handcrafted wand made from natural wood. Go for a walk and look for a detached branch that feels just right. Thank the Tree Spirit before taking the branch. Alternatively, you may know someone who is doing some necessary tree trimming, and you can ask them – and the tree – to help in your quest for a new wand.

While the English woods of ash, hazel, oak or willow are traditional choices, these are fairly difficult to source in Queensland and other parts of Australia. A branch from a beautiful gum tree or nearby cyprus pine works just as well and is rich with the magick of its location.

The usual length of a wand is from index fingertip to elbow, although of course if you prefer a different length, go for it. The wand is always roughly straight, but it can vary in thickness or have knobbly bits with no adverse effects. It should be thin enough to be easily wieldable, and thick enough to have some substance.

To personalise your wand, you may like to:

+ Burn or carve inscriptions of your magical name, runes, ogham or pertinent symbols
+ Attach crystals, feathers, pinecones
+ Anoint it with wax or wood-appropriate, natural oil.

Chalice

This vessel is used for wine or fluid offerings and is symbolic of the Goddess, rebirth, and fertility. It relates to the element of Water and the direction of West.

Your personal chalice is not just your drinking cup as it is a cauldron-on-a-stem. The chalice is ideally made of silver, but of course for most of us this is unrealistic. Glass, clay, pewter, ceramic or metal are practical and readily available choices. You may like to add or engrave moon symbols on your chalice.

If your chalice is made of clear material, it can be used for moon magick by being filled with water, charged with your intentions, and left outside for the night in the moonlight during the full moon. Make sure to retrieve and drink the water before the sun comes up. A chalice can also be used for scrying, although a cauldron or shallow bowl is probably easier to use.

Pentacle

The pentacle is a flat, round piece of brass, gold, silver, wood, clay or glass which is inscribed with a pentagram (five-pointed star). Remember the difference between a pentacle and a pentagram by thinking about the pentacle as a plate.

During ritual, objects are placed on the pentacle for consecration and charging. To economise on altar space, the coven places our plate of cakes upon the pentacle. The pentacle represents the element of Earth and the direction of North.

Other magical tools
Sword
In witchcraft, the sword is the symbol of the coven, rather than an item linked to an individual person. It is used in rituals to cast a circle and banish negative influences. The sword relates to the element of Air and the East, similar to the athame. The only time it is permissible to use a sword for physical cutting is for the cutting of cake during a handfasting ritual.

Censer
The censer is used to burn incense during rituals to welcome good spirits as well as to banish malevolent ones. It represents the element of Air, although it is linked also to Fire. Currently, the coven uses a shallow brass dish to burn loose incense on charcoal discs.

Besom
The besom is a tool sacred to both the Goddess and God, combining a soft brush of bristles with a rigid handle. It can be used to purify and protect a ritual area. While being used to magically sweep or clear a circle, the bristles do not touch the ground. Instead, visualise your besom sweeping away any unnecessary or negative energies to ritually cleanse the area.

A besom can be kept by a door for protection, or put on the ground as a gateway into the ritual space. Couples wishing to be blessed with fecundity jump the broom at handfasting ceremonies, or anyone can jump a besom at Beltane to receive blessings. Besoms are also symbolic of tidiness and cleanliness, and no worthy witch would be without one. Ideally, besoms are made of natural materials, rather than a plastic broom dragged from the depths of the cleaning cupboard.

Cauldron
The cauldron is an ancient vessel of cooking and brew making. It is the container in which magical transformation occurs. The cauldron is associated with renewal, rebirth and inexhaustible plenty.

Traditionally, the cauldron was made of black cast iron, and had three legs. Like the chalice, it is the symbol of the Goddess. I prefer to use a strong, sturdy cauldron so it can be filled with flowers, herbs, water, or fire as circumstances require. A large cauldron is a wonderful focal point for outdoor group rituals, while a mini cauldron is versatile for solitary practitioners and use indoors.

Bell
Ringing a bell unleashes vibrations which can have powerful effects in both the physical and otherworlds. Bells are sometimes rung during ritual to mark important actions, signal significant changes, and declare beginnings and endings. Bells link with the element of Air and feminine energies.

Boline
The boline is a white-handled knife with a curved blade reminiscent of the crescent moon. It is used to cut or carve items. For example, you could use your boline to harvest herbs or carve symbols into candles or talismans.

Staff
Staffs (or stangs) are usually made of wood and are much longer than a wand. From the ground, a staff reaches to waist, shoulder or head height, depending on your personal preference. Similar to the wand, a staff can be used to direct energy, as well as being a tool to clear the path before you, both physically and spiritually.

To acquire your staff, you may feel drawn to buy one which has already been lovingly finished. Having a staff is not a mandatory tool, so please don't feel that you must absolutely have one. Instead of buying one, find or make your own staff. I use a gum tree branch which I found lying on the ground. After stripping off loose bark and trimming both ends, I painted it with oil. It's light and very handy when walking across rough country.

Scourge
The scourge is a whipping device which was traditionally used for beating the dust from household clothing or bedding. In ritual, a scourge may be placed on the altar to remind us of the pain associated with learning or unethical actions.

Mortar and Pestle
The mortar is a strong bowl and the pestle is a sturdy stick; used together, they can grind herbs, seeds, nuts, gums, leaves or minerals.

Consecration Ritual

Consecration is the act of dedicating an item to a sacred use or service. The following rite can be used to help you magically cleanse, consecrate and energise tools, jewellery, talismans or ritual items.

You will need:
- The item you are consecrating
- Lit and smoking incense
- A bowl of water with a pinch of rock salt added.

Ritual:
Cast the circle.

Hold up your item in both hands, high in front of you and say:
Ancient Ones [or call your chosen deity/ancestor/ally]
Creators of all life.
I present my [name of item].
It has been fashioned from the natural world.
It has been wrought into this form.
My will is that it serves me,
As a tool and weapon [or state purpose of item] *in your service.*

Lower your hands to heart level and hold the item within your cupped hands so you can see it.

Dip your fingers into the salted water and sprinkle one side of the item. Turn it over and sprinkle the other side/s and say:
May the cleansing water drive out any impurities from this [name of item]. *May it be cleansed and purified, ready for service. So mote it be.*

Hold the item in the incense smoke, turning so that all parts come in contact with the smoke and say:

May the holy smoke drive out any impurities from this [name of item]. *May it be cleansed and purified, ready for service. So mote it be."*

Hold the item between your palms, focus your energies and say:
I charge this [name of item], *through me and the wisdom and might of the Ancient Ones* [or deity/ancestor/ally].
It will serve me well, protecting me from harm and acting in service of the Mighty Ones, in all things [or add your own wording regarding the purpose of the item]. *So mote it be.*

Take the newly consecrated item to each quarter, starting in the East. Hold it high as you face each of the quarters in turn, saying:
Ye Mighty Ones of the [direction],
Creatures of [Air/Fire/Water/Earth].
This item has been consecrated as tool and weapon of magick [or add your own wording regarding the purpose of the item] *in the presence of the Ancient Ones* [or deity/ancestor/ally]. *So mote it be.*

Close the circle. Eat and drink something to ground yourself.

The Wheel of the Year in the Southern Hemisphere

The Wheel of the Year (WOTY) consists of eight festivals known as sabbats. Witches often mark the passing of the year's cycle by celebrating the associated deities, myths and seasonal changes associated with each sabbat. There are approximately six weeks between each sabbat across a calendar year. The sabbats of Ostara, Litha, Mabon and Yule link to the solar events of equinoxes and solstices, and are commonly called the minor sabbats. The major sabbats (or cross-quarter days) of Lughnasadh, Samhain, Imbolc and Beltane are associated with historical Celtic fire festivals.

Of course, not all witches and Pagans celebrate the WOTY in the same manner and style. It's also difficult to apply northern hemisphere timing to sabbats while living in Australia. The Circle Coven spins the wheel to time sabbats in accordance with our local seasons, moon cycles and astrological timing, rather than stick with the northern hemisphere dates. Australian witches may like to consider regional calendars which have been shared by First Nations peoples. For further information, see the Bureau of Meteorology's *Indigenous Weather Knowledge* site.

I find the modern WOTY system is an effective way to connect with my local environment, as well as with other Pagans during community celebrations. By focussing on seasonal changes, we learn about our internal cycles and can use these connections for active spiritual growth.

> Consider that each sabbat holds within it a mystery which corresponds to the sabbat at the opposite time of the year, for example Samhain / Beltane or Yule / Litha.

The Circle Coven considers sabbats to be celebrations that are ideal for public rituals or for guests to attend, in contrast to esbats (full moon rituals) which we celebrate as intimate, inner-focused rituals that include spellwork. Sabbats usually include dramatic performance and mythic themes, which are integrated into ritual in a practical, participatory manner. For example, at the autumn equinox (Mabon), we may journey to the underworld like the Greek goddess Persephone, or ceremoniously burn a Yule log at midwinter.

History and background of the WOTY

The eight sabbats per year system was introduced in the 1950s. Pre-Christian European people celebrated only at certain times of the year, not on every seasonal or solar occasion. Scholars such as Ronald Hutton (*The Stations of the Sun*) suggest that early Pagan practices varied considerably between locations.

The Wheel of the Year is not one simple, cohesive system, although many Neopagans use it as such. There are a range of myth cycles and components woven through the contemporary WOTY. An example is the theme of a life cycle:

- Death at Samhain
- Birth at Yule (winter solstice)
- Childhood at Imbolc
- Growth at Ostara (spring equinox)
- Fertility at Beltane
- Maturity at Litha (summer solstice)
- Fulfilment at Lughnasadh
- Decline at Mabon (autumn equinox) and back again to death (or descent) and rebirth at Samhain.

These myth cycles are related to archetypal goddess and god motifs. There are also the interplay and impacts of the solar and lunar cycles within the WOTY, which is explored in *The Magic of Time* chapter.

As you work through the annual WOTY cycle, contemplate how aspects of the Gods are within you, just as much as they can seem to be external to you. If you cannot feel the spark of the divine within, you may experience it in a disconnected way; or as malevolent, terrifying; or shadowy and diluted. If you don't turn the cycle within you, you are an observer of outside events rather than a participant in the cosmic dance. By celebrating the changing seasons, we learn about our internal cycles and use these connections for active magical growth.

The Sabbats

Samhain

30 April, or astrologically when the Sun is at 15 degrees Taurus (approximately 6 May).
Major sabbat.

Key points:

- Samhain is pronounced "sow-in" (the first syllable rhymes with cow).
- This sabbat marks the end and beginning of the Pagan year.
- Samhain is considered a time outside of time. The door between the mundane world and the otherworlds is ajar and the veils are thin.
- Notice how close Samhain is to ANZAC day, which is a time Australia collectively remembers and honours the dead and ancestors.
- The God exists only as a seed of potential. The Goddess is crone/hag and sorrows for her sacrificed lover. Mourning, She enters the realm of the dead.

Activities:

- Do some scrying or divination.
- Connect with your ancestors. Place photos or their favourite items on your altar.
- Attend an ANZAC day dawn ceremony.
- Host a dumb supper (a silent dinner to honour the dead).

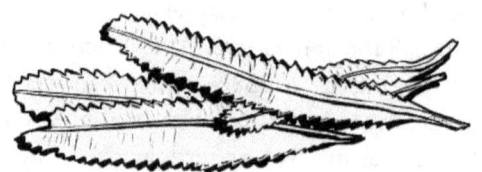

Yule

Midwinter solstice, when the Sun moves into Cancer (approximately 21 June). Minor sabbat.

Key points:
- Yule is the shortest day and longest night of the year.
- The symbolism revolves around rebirth of the Sun/son. The God who was dead lives again.
- The Holly King and Oak King fight for supremacy. The Holly King is defeated and the Oak King rules.
- The Goddess gives birth.

Activities:
- Light a candle in the darkness to represent the return of the sun.
- Decorate a tree with homemade items and shiny adornments.
- Host a midwinter feast for your family and friends.
- Create a Yule log.

Imbolc

1 August, or astrologically when the Sun is at 15 degrees Leo (approximately 7 August).
Major Sabbat.

Key points:

- This sabbat is also called Candlemas.
- The Earth awakens after the winter months.
- Imbolc is first of three festivals celebrating feminine spirituality.
- Brigid's festival of lights. She is the goddess of poetry, healing and smithcraft.
- The Goddess is a maiden. The God is a child.

Practical activities:

- Start a new project or craft.
- Light one or three or nine candles.
- Fill your cauldron (or bathtub) with water and light some floating candles.

Ostara

Spring equinox, when the Sun moves into Libra (approximately 21 September).
Minor sabbat.

Key points:

- ✦ The second of three festivals celebrating feminine spirituality.
- ✦ Celebrates spring and new life.
- ✦ The Goddess is crowned as Spring Queen. The God is on the cusp of manhood.
- ✦ Day and night are even.
- ✦ In the northern hemisphere, this festival is associated with Easter. Despite a popular meme, the goddess Ishtar is not associated with Ostara.

Practical activities:

- ✦ Plant some flowers or herbs. Refer to *A Witch's Apothecary* chapter for some great ideas.
- ✦ Paint or dye eggs.
- ✦ Create a flower crown.

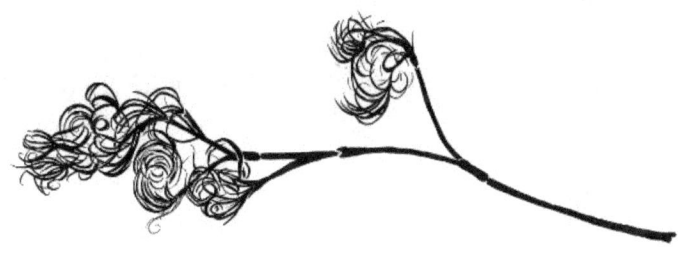

Beltane

31 October, or astrologically when the Sun is at 15 degrees Scorpio (approximately 7 November).
Major Sabbat.

Key points – Beltane:

- ✦ The beginning of summer.
- ✦ A celebration of fertility and delight in lusty, physical pleasures.
- ✦ The Goddess is crowned Queen of Summer. She is mature but not motherly. She is initiatrix. The God is approaching his prime. Can he pass the test to become the King of Summer and be Her consort?
- ✦ Bel fires are lit on the hilltops.
- ✦ In the northern hemisphere, Samhain falls at the end of October. This causes Australian witches some angst, as we want to celebrate Beltane, but the stores are full of cool Halloween costumes and sometimes we need to go trick-or-treating with children.

Practical activities:

- ✦ Safely light a fire or two. Either jump over the flames or walk between them to symbolize passing through a doorway.
- ✦ A good time to conceive children.
- ✦ Leap over a broomstick and make a pledge.
- ✦ Commune with the faeries or local field and forest sprites. Leave offerings of bread and honey.

Litha

Summer solstice, when the Sun moves into Capricorn (approximately 21 December).
Minor sabbat.

Key points:
- This is a masculine festival all about the Sun.
- The Holly King again battles the Oak King, who this time loses the battle.
- It is the longest day and shortest night of the year.

Practical activities:
- Soak up the warmth. Don't do anything too intense.
- Go to the beach.
- Be kind to yourself in the lead up to the 'silly season'.
- Stay up all night to greet the rising of the sun.

Lughnasadh

1 or 2 February or astrologically when the Sun is at 15 degrees Aquarius (approximately 4 February).
Major sabbat.

Key points:

- ✦ Some Pagans name this sabbat Lammas.
- ✦ This is the first harvest festival. Everything is full of life.
- ✦ The King marries the Queen of the Land. In marriage, He prepares to be sacrificed, as He will die at the autumn equinox.

Practical activities:

- ✦ Tie up loose ends and complete projects.
- ✦ Decorate your ritual altar with seasonally ripe, local fruits and vegetables.
- ✦ Make time for games and competitive sports – in accordance with the myth relating to Taitu, the mother of Lugh.
- ✦ Make a contract with yourself to achieve your goals over the next year.

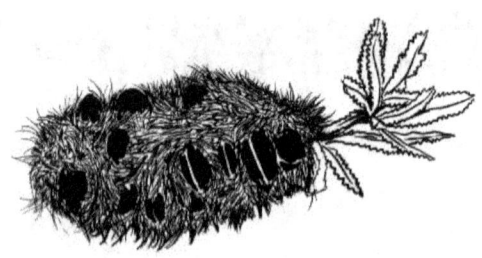

Mabon

Autumn equinox, when the Sun moves into Aries (approximately 21 March). Minor sabbat.

Key points:
- The name Mabon only became associated with the autumn equinox in the 1970s, and some Pagans prefer to not to use it.
- The second harvest festival.
- The theme of sacrifice continues. The Corn King or Barley King must die so that the people can live.
- It is a time to celebrate the culmination of hard work.
- Days and nights are evenly balanced.

Practical activities – Mabon:
- Decorate your ritual altar with freshly harvested fruits and vegetables.
- Create a meal using flour or wheat as base (for example, bread) and share with your family or loved ones.
- Craft a ritual rattle from a gourd.

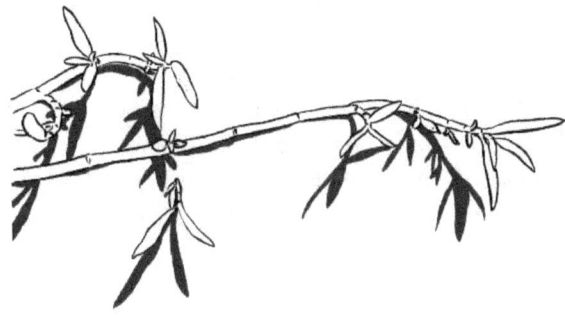

Deity: Goddess, God and the Gods

Except for atheistic or agnostic witches, contemporary witches tend to follow one or more of the following belief systems: pantheism, duotheism or polytheism. Let's look at each of these.

Pantheism

Witches who are pantheists believe there is a greater consciousness or spirit which is within us, around us and outside of us that causes, creates and connects everything that has been, everything that is and everything that will be. It's not possible to fully comprehend this greater consciousness because it is so huge and complex and unknowable. However, at times, you feel a sense of connection, as if you are in tune (or at times, out of step) with a vast universal dance. This incomprehensible 'thing' has been called many names, including 'the Universe,' the Goddess, Spirit, the divine, the numinous, the force, or our higher selves.

Because we also contain a spark of it within us, we are always connected to that greater wholeness. Pantheists believe that the divine is not separate from the physical world. This notion is called immanence, which links to a concept called animism. Many modern witches and magick-workers believe all things are imbued with and energised by this spirit – even items such as cars and computers.

Duotheism

> *'All gods are one God, and all goddesses are one Goddess, and there is only one Initiator.'*
> Dion Fortune, in *The Sea Priestess*.

For women, the concept of duotheism can be liberating, as the divine feminine is regarded as equal to the divine masculine, rather than considered inferior or ignored completely as it is in monotheistic traditions.

Many witches honour the Great Goddess (feminine principle) in threefold archetypal forms, seeing Her as being three separate, yet connected, aspects. The most common traits associated with triplicate aspects of the Goddess are:

+ **Maiden.** Young woman. Waxing moon. Spring. Innocence, new beginnings and the colour white.
+ **Mother.** Mature woman. Full moon. Summer. Lover, childbirth, experience, creativity and the colour red.
+ **Crone.** Old age. Waning moon. Autumn. Wisdom, decline and the colour black.

As these are archetypes, physical age is fluid. You can be a young person and have attributes of the Crone. Nor do you need to have given birth to embrace the Mother archetype.

Within The Circle Coven, we honour the Great Goddess in quadruple form. We include a fourth aspect of the Goddess, that of ***The Silent One***, She of the new/dark moon. Her face is hidden. She is the void, that space in the dance between endings and beginnings. She is the potentiate. This is the ancient one who is the destroyer, but without her we would not have new life and beginnings. Hers is the darkness of the withered womb, and of the still chalice filled with quiescent poison. Her realm is that of the hidden and the forbidden; the secrets which are kept unto death. Her power lies in silence.

While this quadruple aspecting could be unique to The Circle Coven – developed over decades of ritual work – we certainly aren't the first or only witches to associate the Goddess with four aspects rather than in triple form.

The universal Great God (masculine principle) also has a range of archetypal associations. There is the dualistic concept of the Oak King and the Holly King, the opponents who challenge each other through the cycle of the year. At the height of summer, the Oak King reigns supreme, having killed the weakened Holly King. But at the height of winter, the Oak King is slain in turn, only to re-emerge again to fight the Holly King at the time of the summer solstice.

The masculine archetypes favoured by The Circle Coven include the Horned God, the hunter who is aligned with the beasts and creatures of the wild forest places. He is primal, raw, sexual and instinctual. He may appear as part-man, part-beast. The other key Great God archetype we integrate into coven practice is the Green Man, the masculine force associated with earthy growth and vegetation. He is gentle, but also radiates strong vitality. Instead of animal horns, branches might emerge from the crown of his head.

Polytheism – the Gods

It might sound masculinely gendered when we talk of 'the Gods'. However, this term means the enormous range of masculine, feminine and diverse individual divine beings who have been worshipped and honoured by humans for thousands of years. To learn about and connect with the Gods, we look to mythology, legends or archaeological evidence whose origins are not in the religions of the 'people of the book' (i.e., Christians, Muslims or Jews).

To work with individual gods, you need to connect to the essence, characteristics and history of that godform. Witches do this for many reasons, particularly if we feel called to form a bond with a specific goddess or god. There's more information about this in the *How to Connect with a Patron Deity* chapter. Another reason for connecting with the Gods is their archetypal energies. An example of working with archetypal energies is to call upon the qualities of Athena for assistance when you require a calm mind to make wise judgements.

A warning: The Gods aren't necessarily kind, benign, easy spirits, who are conveniently summoned on a whim to help you and pat you kindly on the head like a fond, loving parent. They are immense energies in themselves as well as conduits to immensity. You should research thoroughly (and form a relationship) before calling upon any deity. For example, Cerridwen may be seen as a mother figure by some, but she can also be a devouring Sow Goddess and Initiator.

If you include more than one deity in a ritual, for added harmony include compatible deities from the same background or pantheon.

As witches, we don't really 'worship' the Gods. This is because there is the spark of deity within each of us. What we do instead, is honour and respect the Gods. We can also celebrate them by singing, dancing, listening, being respectful, providing appropriate offerings and symbols (for example, a horse statue on your altar for Epona) and by involving them in our everyday activities.

Mythologies

History is written by the conquerors, which means most of the early European myths and stories were transcribed and translated by male Christians. This led to a patriarchal slant in some texts, where goddesses are relegated as consorts, portrayed as villains, or occupy lesser supporting roles. Fortunately, there are contemporary authors who are reclaiming the voices of the divine feminine from ancient literature.

This is just one challenge in accessing accurate information about pre-Christian gods. Over time, and between locations, the names, roles and functions of the Gods also can change. This adds another layer of complexity when we try to understand the myth cycles and qualities of particular gods. Some gods have also been made into saints by the church (for example, St Brigid), or perhaps diminished into creatures such as leprechauns.

Below are some starting points for learning about gods and goddesses from six major Western pre-Christian cultures.

Mesopotamian

- Timeframe: 3500 BC – 400 AD approximately
- Location: Iraq, Kuwait, Turkey, Syria
- Read: *The Epic of Gilgamesh*
- Check out: The Igigi, Anunnaki and the descent of Inanna
- Deities: Inanna/Ishtar, Anu, Enlil, Enki/Ea, Sin, Marduk, Ereshkigal.

Celtic

- Location: primarily Ireland, Scotland, Wales
- Read: *The Mabinogion, The Books of Dun Cow, The Book of Ballymore*
- Check out: Sidhe, Druids
- Deities: Dagda, Danu, Lugh, Nuada, Brigit, Cerridwen, Rhiannon, Morrigan, Cernunnos.

Egyptian

- Location: Egypt
- Read: books by Donald B. Redford, David O'Connor or Manfred Lurker
- Check out: Pyramids, creation myths
- Deities: Isis, Osiris, Sekhmet, Set, Anubis, Nuit, Hathor, Geb.

Nordic/Teutonic

- Location: Germany, Scandinavia and throughout northern Europe
- Read: *Edda* (poetry and prose)
- Check out: Aesir, Vanir, Sleipnir, Valkyries

- Deities: Odin, Loki, Thor, Tyr, Freya, Hel.

Greek and Roman
- Location: Mediterranean
- Read: *The Odyssey* (by Homer), *The Metamorphoses* (by Ovid), Ancient Greek drama (from the bawdy comedy *Lysistrata* to tragedies such as *Oedipus Rex* and *Medea*)
- Check out: How pop culture has integrated Greek and Roman mythology
- Deities: Zeus/Jupiter, Hera/Juno, Poseidon/Neptune, Demeter/Ceres, Ares/Mars, Artemis/Diana, Athena/Minerva, Hephaestus/Vulcan, Aphrodite/Venus, Dionysius/Bacchus, Hades/Pluto, Hestia/Vesta. Apollo.

How to Connect with a Patron Deity

Beginner witches sometimes ask about patron deities and how to connect with a particular goddess or god. Do they choose you? How do you choose a god to work with? How do you know if they are the right deity for you and what are the signs that you both vibe together?

These are all fantastic questions.

Connecting with a particular goddess or god is very much like starting a relationship with a person. For example, maybe you hook up with an interesting person within 30 minutes via an online dating app. You meet, have a physical connection, then bam! Gone. Bye, Felicia. Maybe the meeting was satisfactory on some temporary level, but it's certainly not on the same level as a loving, long-term relationship that has stood the test of time.

It's the same when connecting with a deity. The more work you put into building a relationship, the better the outcomes and the stronger the connection. Of course, sometimes it is immediate love (or lust) at first sight, and there you are, 50 years later, with more grandchildren than you can poke a stick at. But not everyone has the same results on every occasion.

As you would when seeking to enter a new relationship, take stock of yourself. What are your strengths? What are your weaknesses? What are your idiosyncrasies? What's missing from your life and what do you have in abundance? Most importantly, what do you love and cherish on a deeper level? What keeps you in amazement and awe? What drives you forward and delights you? What is your family background, and where do you live? What level of commitment are you able to provide? Your answers to these questions offer clues that could lead to your potential patron deity.

Sometimes, something just clicks and you find you have a particular interest in a being, though you may not know their name at first. It could seem quite irrational to your conscious mind, as there might be a sudden epiphany or hints are revealed through repeated dreams. Or you might start to see themes or recurring patterns which previously weren't obvious or held only limited meaning. Maybe it's an image that caught your eye, or a phrase, or a symbol.

Through any of these means, one or more deities will be revealed to you. You may feel a strong interest or bond with them, or just be insatiably curious to know more. Most deities are pretty keen to get to know you too, in their own distinctive way. Which leads us to the question: does a deity choose you or do you choose them? I think, like any healthy relationship, it's a two-way process, though forming a bond with some deities can be difficult as they are naturally less communicative or just not that interested in you.

Can you reject the advances of a deity who comes knocking at your door, who is just begging you to honour and revere them? Absolutely. Like any good relationship, you have the right to say "no." Sometimes it's just too much for you right now due to the demands of your everyday life – you might not have the time or energy to honour the intensity of this sacred relationship. Or you might feel intuitively that it's not right. Or perhaps you've already sworn to one or more deities and the workload is just too much. Don't laugh too much at that – it's a real consideration in the life of a busy witch. Likewise, the deity might not be too impressed by you either, or you may not fit the criteria for what they require right now.

Now you've got a potential deity in mind (or They have stepped forward and claimed you), what do you do next?

As in a good relationship, it's all about building connection. Do the work. Do your research. Read about the myths associated with that deity, preferably from a reputable translation. Learn about the cultural context, their relationship with other gods, and what they like and dislike. You give to the god; They give back to you. You might like to provide offerings which appeal to them (I will never forget a ritual honouring Sekhmet which featured an animal heart), or create an altar and meditate at it. Seek out artwork (ancient and modern) to display Their image in a suitable format. Try to avoid the hypersexualised, big tit, fantasy figures of fan-boy art, unless of course the deity is really into that.

And, of course, while you are doing all of these things you are spending time, effort and energy focused towards Them. Connecting, connecting, connecting. After that connection has been formed, when you need support, it's easy to link in with that deity because you have a calling card, and they know who you are. It's a reciprocal, and healthy association founded on good manners, time spent together, trust and understanding. The power of this mutually beneficial spiritual relationship can (almost) move mountains and certainly help you withstand a storm.

Like any relationship, sometimes you have to provide boundaries and balance. Within our coven practices, we will sometimes work with particular goddesses and gods for a defined time period. We do this by forming agreements that the intense relationship will morph into a friend-zone space further down the line. Naturally, things don't work out like this all the time, but if that particular goddess or god is creating unwelcome havoc or unhelpful outcomes, there might come a time to say "farewell" or take a mutual break. And that's a reasonable thing to do.

A word here about the cultural appropriation of deity. This is a very sensitive matter, to which there is no universally correct answer. I feel that I'm treading on eggshells trying to give a reasonable answer, but here goes. I don't believe people are forbidden to learn about and associate with beings/deity from cultural or ancestral backgrounds different to their own. For example, I certainly would never dream of gate-keeping British deities from someone with South American ancestry. The gods themselves reach out in strange and mysterious ways and don't appear to be constrained by physical location, skin colour, body type or cultural practices.

But this is not the same as learning about or practicing a closed cultural tradition, such as Haitian Vodou or Indigenous spiritual traditions. If you feel the need to align with a deity who is part of a closed cultural tradition (and a simple internet search will let you know if this is the case), I suggest you politely approach someone who works with that system and respectfully ask for guidance. And a heads-up, the fact that you might have been invited to witness a closed cultural event does not give you permission to use any part of that tradition. It is particularly inappropriate to benefit financially from knowledge of a closed cultural tradition to which you do not belong.

FACETS: Witchery Lore

This section includes a range of topics and lore relevant to witchcraft. It also features chapters by invited guest authors, who are experienced magic-workers living in Australia.

Image by Jae Arnell

The constellation known as Antares (α Scorpii) is called Djuit by the Boorong people of Victoria. Djuit is the name for the red-rumped parrot in Boorong language. He is the son of Marpeankurrk, which is Arcturus (α Boötis). The faint stars at either side of Antares are Djuit's wives. ~ Chadrac

Sky Yarning – Indigenous Astronomy

By Chadrac Sloane

Indigenous Australians are astronomers. Well, perhaps astronomer is not the correct term, as they did a lot more than just watch the stars and planetary shifts. But in this chapter, we will refer to it as Indigenous Astronomy.

Dated ancient stone constructions show that Indigenous people were observing and recording the sky, the stars, and the movements of the planets long before the Babylonians, Egyptians, and Greeks. Across the many varying Indigenous communities across what is now known as Australia, each and every nation has stories and actions based on the understandings of the various types of astronomical phenomena that are visible in the southern skies. The Traditional Owners and Elders know how to read the stars, they know the dances, and they can sing all the relevant songs to the stars. But the stories are not just simply about the songs and the stars. It is much, much more than that.

The horizon is not a line that separates earthly life from that of the static atmosphere above; in contrast, the horizon is the glue that holds the universe together. The stories that are told in the stars provide a constantly reliable source for following the natural cycles of life. Indigenous people have observed the night sky for thousands of years, and their observations led to an established and stable society based on the natural environs with communities that had social expectations founded in what was seen, what was felt and what changed over long periods of time. These stories were also used to explain ethics, for illustrating points, for understanding and for the reiteration of the rule-based society that is known as Lore.

The ancient sacred stories tell of creators who came from the Earth and then created everything upon it; upon completion they then returned back to the land or there were some that went to the Skyland. There is a circular understanding of life and the inner workings of traditional customary ways of life. This perspective and ideology are effective ways of protecting nature, by providing a powerful link between humans, plants, and wildlife and that which is beyond. It helps us, as humans, to look behind our veils of human-centric ignorance and social conditioning, and to more broadly understand the needs of other creatures and ecosystems more deeply and more empathetically.

The stories of Western astrology, especially those of the movement of the lights of the night sky, are familiar to many people (and covered in next chapter, *The Magic of Time*). However, the stories that are Indigenous to the southern skies are less well known. Although it must be noted that different First Nations groups across the land have different astronomical traditions, it must be recognised that there are also some broad similarities between many of the traditional language groupings.

Similarities include things like the changing night skies mirroring seasonal patterns in the activities of animals and plants. Astronomical events can be messages about events soon to happen on the ground. In many cases, the landscape on the earthly horizon itself is seen as a reflection of the patterns in the night sky. Additionally, these important indicators of the sky world are representative of crucial seasonal changes that are vital to land custodianship, food sourcing and availability.

Indigenous Australians also used the stars of the sky world for navigation, ceremony, and cultural traditions that continue today. Indigenous Australians have been developing complex knowledge systems for tens of thousands of years and passing this information on through the art of oral storytelling. These traditional stories can be seen in ancient cave paintings, many of which are related to the Skyland.

Luckily, some of these stories have survived through time. There are many researchers and Indigenous groups working together to bring to light the rich cultural and scientific history we have here in Australia. As with other ancient cultural traditions across the globe, Indigenous Australian astronomy is important not just for its own sake, but for the holistic approach taken by Indigenous people and the understanding and knowing that the night sky was and is an enveloping landscape that is integrated and flows with all forms of traditional knowledge and Lore.

The connections between the night sky of the stars above, the terrestrial land upon which we walk, and the underworld below were and still are crucial parts of Indigenous cosmology and culture. Astrological events and influences from the cosmic landscape have a significant role in the ordering of all life for First Nations people. The observable seasonal changes that can be seen in the cosmos due to the movement of planets and constellations are mimicked by the terrestrial movements of people, plants, and animals. These observances have strengthened and solidified that the cosmos is indeed a landscape.

These cosmic regions were considered by Aboriginal people to be part of the land that they are the custodians of. A social kinship system linked many of the celestial bodies, the cosmos, and all earthly landscapes. The stars teach the stories and reinforce culture, the cosmos offers reference points to indicate important aspects of, and expected, cultural and lifestyle actions. For example, Orion's Belt and the Seven Sisters are symbolic of a story that is used to teach and reinforce the importance of the traditional marriage system. Another story from the night sky that determines lifestyle and cultural practices is the tradition of the Emu in the Sky.

This story is of great importance to many Indigenous groups. The Emu in the Sky stretches across the Milky Way in the southern night sky. To see the Emu, look closely at the Southern Cross and you will see the Emu's head as a dark smudge tucked near the bottom left-hand corner of the constellation. As you look, concentrate on the mass of dark clouds, and not at the bright stars and you will see the Emu within the darkness. The position of the Emu, as it moves across each section of the night sky, determines the right time to do things (such as breeding time and safe collection of emu eggs) and knowing that the right time to do this was to sustain the most fragile of ecosystems. There are many other stories and vital Lore intertwined with the night sky. You can find out more about the Emu in the Sky at <http://emudreaming.com>

Not only do Traditional Owners know the sky intimately, but they are also well versed in the cross-quarters, planetary motion, tides, and eclipses. There are, still to this day, solar observatories built in stone. These were created by First Nations groups and are used to mark the time of the year by the solstices and are sacred places of ceremony. The Traditional songs and stories show how First Nations people understand their Universe in a scientific way. Using the knowledge of observations of the sky world to construct calendars and timing systems, as well as navigational tools that enabled long-distance navigation across the country, and sea, whilst trading artefacts and sharing sacred stories.

Indigenous people have and still use their knowledge of the night sky to forecast the weather, determine seasonal changes and to make predictions. Torres Strait Islanders use the scintillation of stars (twinkling) to determine when the northwest monsoon is arriving. Some southern-based First Nations groups used the ice rings around the moon to forecast when wet weather was arriving. They also know that the arrival of the Seven Sisters in the evening sky brought the return of warm weather and lots of resources, while their setting in the evening sky brought the dark and cold changes that come with winter.

Perhaps you would like to acknowledge the Skyland into your practice. Considerate ways you can do this include beginning your own personal land journal. Start to record and observe the changes and effects that each of the moon phases has on your own personal space and biosphere. Take notes of the daily weather and its patterns, record what the animals are doing, what birds come and go. Are they nesting or foraging? Are there any young? Note down the growth and activity of plants. What is blooming, shooting, or going dormant?

Also remember to take night-time notes in your journal too. Spend time at night observing the sky and the stars within it. This is how you will be able to observe and correlate the relationships between the elements of the cosmos in its entirety in your notes. Once you feel you have understood the moon cycles, you could move on to further investigate the sky land by observing and recording star groupings and by tracking movements.

This stargazing may include activities such as pulling all-nighters and rising from your warm slumbers in winter to observe the sky before the sun breaches the eastern horizon. Do not forget to take notes in your journal of the constellations that you are drawn to. The night sky is enchanting, and many times I have not finished my planned notes or sketch of a star grouping because I'm fully caught in the moment. In preparation, you may like to set aside some time for reflection and journaling after the stargazing moment. Allow yourself to be fully present in the stargazing, as it can be truly wonderful and moving.

The Magic of Time

By Kim Fairminer

Astrology is a rich symbolic language and an incredibly versatile tool for the modern witch. It's my preferred divination method, and an indispensable part of my everyday life.

As you might expect from an occult science that is thousands of years old and has endured the rise and fall of many empires, astrology is a complex system. You certainly won't pick up a working understanding of astrology via memes and magazine horoscopes (or indeed, this chapter), any more than you can fully assess the quality of a romantic prospect through their online dating profile alone.

That said, you probably already know more than you think you do. Assessing the quality of a potential lover (or anyone else) based their 'star sign' is a crude form of natal astrology. Unless you were born on the cusp (towards the boundary of a zodiacal sign) you can confidently work out your Sun sign. You probably know a thing or two about some of the other Sun signs through your interactions with your family, friends, and workmates.

As a witch, timing your spells with the days of the week or the phases of the Moon is basic yet vital astrological magic. Choosing an auspicious time to enhance the results of a magical or mundane activity is called electional astrology. Natal and electional astrology are two of the four branches of astrology. The other two branches are horary astrology, a divinatory practice that casts a chart for the moment of the question, and mundane astrology, which studies the natural world and collective human endeavours.

Becoming a proficient astrologer takes many years of dedicated study and practice. Fortunately, you don't need to be able to read an astrological chart to tap into the magic of time. This chapter will help you get started with integrating astrology into your witchery.

Sorting the wheat from the chaff (or getting your Virgo on)

In recent years, the internet has exploded with a wealth of astrological content. There are many excellent resources available for free; there's also a lot of plagiarism, nonsensical memes, blatant misinformation, and wannabe gurus trying to turn a quick profit.

I have spent decades and lots of money studying astrology. I have immersed myself in stacks of books. I have sat enthralled by the words of learned scholars. I have travelled to foreign lands to increase my understanding. I have tied my mind in knots over big philosophical questions and slowly unravelled them again. And still, I have barely scratched the surface of the wonder that is astrology.

When I see nonsense masquerading as astrology, written by someone who obviously didn't look in an ephemeris (and probably doesn't know what one is), it makes me sad. There are plenty of astrologers – even astrology students – who would've helped. Misleading, and often sensationalist, information is widely circulated through social media and it brings all metaphysical practitioners into disrepute.

By all means, have fun. Also, be discerning.

As you read this chapter, keep your expectations reasonable. You aren't going to learn it all right here, right now. More broadly, this principle applies to your practice of witchcraft, as well as astrology. It's a lifelong journey of discovery.

Be warned: you now teeter on the edge of a magical universe. You could lose your balance and begin the deep and dizzying tumble down the astrological rabbit hole.

Time as a magical tool

'What is the above is from the below and the below is from the above. The work of wonders is from one.'
The Emerald Tablet translated by Nineveh Shadrach.
<www.scribd.com/document/126171303/Emerald-Tablet>

The efficacy of your spellwork depends not only on your own magical prowess, but also the time that you do the working. Put simply: it's not all about you. As a witch, you work with natural cycles – and, in my experience, nature extends well beyond planet Earth.

The right spell at the wrong time will hinder your success rate, so if you want your magic to get the desired results, add astrology to your magical toolkit. While there is no such thing as perfect timing, astrology will give your spells a boost. Between lunar phase, zodiacal signs, planetary hours and more, you have plenty of celestial support to reach your magical goals.

Time is my go-to magical ingredient. It's readily available, easy to carry, and packs serious punch.

I'm not talking about the quantified seconds and minutes on a clock though. That's chronus. I'm talking about the *quality* of time: kairos. Kairos is a Greek word for the opportune moment. No doubt you have experienced it yourself. Perhaps you've let important opportunities slip by; like in the film, *Sliding Doors*. Those split-second moments when a decision is made, when you say your piece (or not), when you leap to an action that you have put off for years and it's the best thing you've ever done and you wonder why it took you so long.

These moments matter because every single moment in space and time has a particular quality or energy. This is why your natal chart, which is a snapshot of the skies at your birth, is considered a blueprint of your life.

Astrology is the language we use to explore the quality of time. It empowers you to engage with the magic of the Universe.

Perhaps you've already leapt in and experienced the wonder of casting a circle by the light of the Full Moon. Or gazed upon the Milky Way arched above you on a clear, dark night. Our lives on Earth are intimately tied to the movements of our closest heavenly bodies – our closest star, the Sun, and Earth's satellite, the Moon. The Moon and Sun, of course, aren't the only heavenly bodies relevant to our existence here on Earth. Keeping up-to-date on major astrological transits is a fundamental principle for empowering your spellwork – and it has been so for thousands of years.

Choosing your handfasting date is deserving of much more time, skill, and patience than waiting for the planetary hour to tick over before you flick off an offer on a second-hand find.

Sometimes it's worth waiting for the optimum time, other times you just need to get it done.

Seasons and cycles

Whether you're into folk music or the bible:

> *'For everything there is a season, and a time for every matter under heaven.'*
> Ecclesiastes 3:1, The Bible (KJV)

The stars are not some far-off fantasy, they impact everything we do every day. Life here on Earth probably came from the stars. Neolithic people recorded celestial movements, including the movements of fixed stars (which enabled them to migrate across oceans) and the impact of meteors. All cultures across the globe, across time, have star myths. As human beings, our stories are the stories of the stars.

The Sun and the Moon are our luminaries, the givers of light to our Earth. The Sun gives light during the day; the Moon gives light at night. They are our primary cosmic representatives of the masculine and feminine archetypes. The Sun and the Moon are the source of life and our measure of time. They give us the seasons, the tides, day and night.

The dance between the Sun and the Moon is still encapsulated in the modern Gregorian calendar because – even with our environmental impact and our technological advancements – the Sun and Moon are fundamental to our existence here on Earth.

It's easy to forget that the Sun is our closest star, which warms and illuminates us. Without it there would be no life; there would be no seasons. One year is the time Earth takes to do a full circuit around the Sun. This is the solar cycle. We experience this as seasonal change, from summer, to autumn, to winter, and spring and round again. You celebrate the rebirth of your own personal solar cycle every birthday.

"Many happy returns!"
Have you ever wondered what this common birthday greeting means? It's astrological. Every year, the Sun returns to the exact same position as it is in your natal chart. Your birthday is your solar return. Each year, you are reinfused with the light, warmth, and vitality of the Sun.
That's definitely worthy of celebration.

A single month follows the cycle of the Moon. The words 'month' and 'moon' share the same etymological roots. We look to the sky and see the Moon grow and disappear. This is the lunar cycle. The Moon is our closest planetary body and is distinct in that she orbits Earth, rather than the Sun. The Moon moves the tides, and influences the fertility and growth of life on Earth.

Western astrology is based on the tropical zodiac. This means that the zodiacal signs are linked to the annual movement of the Earth around the Sun. The equinoxes and the solstices occur at the beginning of four specific signs of the zodiac every year. These are the cardinal signs of Aries, Cancer, Libra and Capricorn; ancient astrologers called them 'movable' or 'turning' because these signs indicated quick changes. Anchoring the placement of the zodiacal signs with the equinoxes and solstices roots Western tropical astrology firmly on the Earth – perfect for witches.

It's important to remember that the zodiacal signs describe a 30-degree area of *sky*. Although the names of the signs have the same names as constellations, due to the slow wobble of the Earth's rotation (called the precession of the equinoxes), the alignment between the signs and the constellations shifts on a 26,000-year cycle. If the signs were to follow the constellations, as they do in the Hindu/Vedic tradition, the southern autumn equinox would currently occur with the Sun in Pisces, not Aries.

Solar and lunar cycles

The strength of the Sun waxes and wanes throughout the year, although this cycle is more subtle than the ever-changing faces of the Moon. From winter to summer, solar light waxes, and from summer to winter, it wanes. Halfway between the solstice peaks of maximum light and maximum darkness, there are times of balance between night and day at the equinoxes. This cycle is celebrated as key points on the Wheel of the Year,

The ancient Celts (who influenced the modern Wheel of the Year) developed calendars that combined the solar and lunar cycles. The oldest of these is the Coligny calendar, which had twelve months that started with the same lunar phase and added an extra month every 2.5 years to align the lunations with the solar year. The Celts divided their year into a light half and a dark half. Although not exactly aligned with the solar cycle – the dark half of the Celtic year started at Samhain and ended at Beltane – both Celtic days and years began with the arrival of darkness.

The light half of the solar year and the monthly lunar cycle indicates:
- ✦ Stronger health and vitality
- ✦ Quicker recovery from illness and setbacks
- ✦ An extroverted, outgoing disposition
- ✦ Orientation towards group and public activities
- ✦ External, outward and visible qualities.

The dark half of the solar year and monthly lunar cycles indicates:
- ✦ Increased awareness of effort
- ✦ Extra care to maintain health and vitality
- ✦ An introspective, introverted disposition
- ✦ A focus on mystery, magic, and healing
- ✦ Lower profile, reduced visibility, hidden qualities.

The Moon, more obviously than the Sun, also follows a waxing and waning cycle. It is the relative position of the Sun and the Moon that forms the lunar phases. The Moon moves much quicker than the Sun. In one solar year, the Moon will make 13 revolutions of the zodiac. Or, to view the difference in speed from the Moon's perspective, each month the Sun moves through one 30-degree sign while the Moon moves through all signs of the 360-degree zodiac. Each zodiacal month, there is a New Moon and a Full Moon.

The Moon's phases show the unfolding relationship between the conscious spirit (Sun) and the embodied soul (Moon) – both of which are present within you. It is rewarding to track your menstrual cycle (if you have one), creativity, and emotions with the waxing and waning of the Moon. Staying in touch with the phases of the Moon is staying in touch with the Goddess within, regardless of your gender identity.

New Moons are widely regarded as an optimum time for setting intentions. I like to wait until I see the newly revealed Moon in the western sky just after sunset before I start something new.

The New Moon – which is not visible in the sky because it is so close to the brightness of the Sun – is great for meditation and having that initial moment of realisation.

However, the Crescent Moon offers gentle light and fertile conditions for growth to develop that New Moon vision and bring it to manifestation.

Most witches recognise four lunar phases when planning magical workings – New Moon, waxing, Full Moon, waning. The Moon is a witch's primary calendar for rituals and for life. There's nuance to the waxing and waning stages of the Moon cycle that become apparent when considering the amount of light available and the seasonal correspondence. For this reason, astrologers widely recognise eight different Moon phases instead of four.

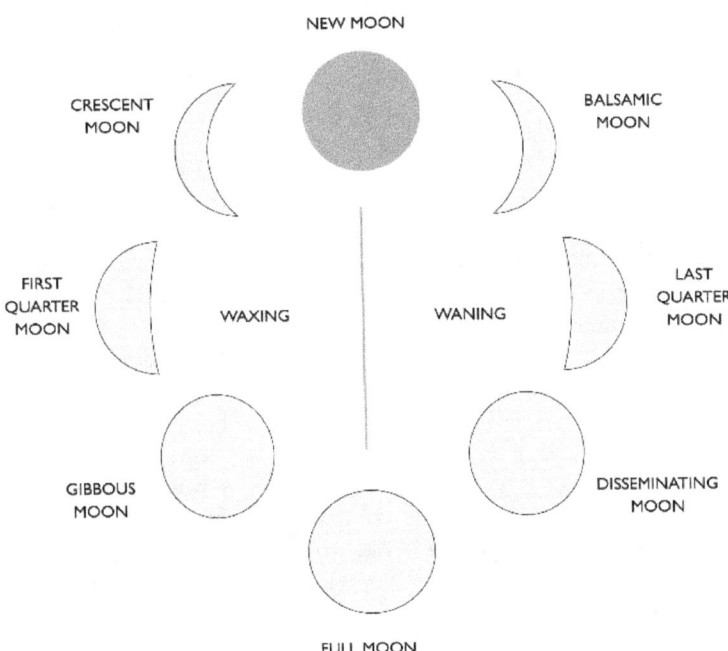

Moon cycles

The eight phases of the Moon share common themes with the corresponding sabbat (seasonal celebration) on the Wheel of the Year. The following table provides correspondences between the Moon phase, sabbats and themes:

Moon phase	Sabbat	Light/ Dark	Themes	Concepts
New	Yule/ Winter Solstice	Light begins in absolute darkness	Begin	- Conception, birth, incarnation, turning point, divine child - First glimmer of light in the darkness - Evergreen, enduring.
Crescent	Imbolc	Darkness retreats, light quickens	Emerge	- Light, bright, innovation, initiation, purity, hope - New thoughts & projects; confirmation of your path for this cycle - Concentrate on the self & development, study, self-contemplation & general introspection.
First quarter	Ostara/ Spring Equinox	Light & dark equal, light gaining	Outward challenge, push	- Awakening, growth, resurgence, transition, renewal - Celebration of life, dual themes of rebirth/sacrifice, light & dark in balance - Take action. Push for progress on your goals for the cycle.
Gibbous	Beltane	Light dominant	Prepare & refine	- Excitement, desire, passion, creativity, anticipation - Elevating personal ideals, desires, & abilities - Examining notions of perfection.
Full	Litha/ Summer Solstice	Absolute light	Peak exposure	- Culmination, peak, climax, fulfilment, *carpe diem* - Light peaks, but this is also the moment that darkness begins to grow - Appreciate the wonder of life & experience

				- Celebrate everything that fulfils you & brings you joy
- Full expression, revelation of the potential of the current cycle.
Dissemi nating	Lugh- nasadh	Light retreats, darkness quickens	Share	- Harvest, abundance, achievement, generosity, afterglow
- Assess your achievements & personal harvest
- Share your knowledge, teach what you've learned
- Fruition of the cycle, prepare to let go & enter darkness
- Preserve meaning for next cycle.
Last quarter	Mabon/ Autumn Equinox	Light & dark equal, darkness gaining	Inner challenge, truth	- Gratitude, gathering, sorting, storing, pruning
- Preparation for darkness & decline
- Accepting the harvest that will sustain you through the dark half of the cycle
- End of hard work, time to start 'recharging your batteries'
- Reorientation from external to internal activities.
Balsamic	Samhain	Darkness dominates & overcomes light	Release & retreat	- Death, ending, loss, release, transformation, insight, mystery
- Recognition & celebration of life & death
- Contemplation of the past & assessment of that cycle's progress
- Connecting with the ancestors, facing the shadow, dark emotions.

Planetary magic

In addition to working with the cycles of the Sun and the Moon, you can work magick with the planets.

When we speak of 'planets' in astrology, it usually includes the Sun, the Moon, and celestial bodies that aren't considered to be planets according to astronomical definitions. Each planet represents a particular kind of energy, which you will tend to experience and express as instinctive drives or urges.

Like the Moon, planets also have phases. For example, when a planet cojoins (lines up with) the Sun, it is like a New Moon for that planet, signifying the beginning of a new cycle.

Here are some key words for the planets to get you started:

Sun. The essential self, identity, will, life purpose, vitality, conscious self-expression.

Moon. The instinctual self, habits, moods, nourishment, mothering, home, roots, the past.

Mercury. Awareness, thought processes, learning, communication, curiosity, reason.

Venus. Attraction, relationship, harmony, beauty, pleasure, artistry.

Mars. Assertion, independence, action, competition, conflict, courage, initiative.

Jupiter. Expansion, faith, luck, belief, travel, exploration, exaggeration.

Saturn. Limitation, structure, discipline, boundaries, responsibility, caution.

Uranus. Liberation, freedom, idealism, revolution, rebellion, shock.

Neptune. Transcendence, inspiration, imagination, disintegration, self-sacrifice, unconsciousness.

Pluto. Crisis, annihilation, intensity, manipulation, compulsion, decay, obsession.

Each planet has significations that are specific to your own natal chart, which you can learn about through further study or during a consultation with a professional astrologer. Planets are sometimes in a better position to help you than at other times. When a planet is in their home sign, they are strong and well resourced. When a planet is an honoured guest in the sign of its exaltation (i.e. strengthened), it is in a very good mood and also able to help. When a planet is far from home (in detriment or fall), the planet is in unfamiliar territory and isn't able to assist you much.

Another example of planetary condition is when a planet is retrograde, or (in simple terms) appears to be moving backwards in the sky. Retrograde movements also impact on spell workings. For example, creating a talisman for persuasive speech during Mercury retrograde is highly unlikely to get the results you desire.

To further understand the associations of each planet, I recommend that you research the deity that the planet is named after. From the mythological stories about each deity, you will learn more about each planet. This will then help you to layer symbolism in your spellwork, as well as to gain the favour of that particular god or goddess by using appropriate offerings on your altar.

Building a relationship with each of the planets through regular offerings and devotion over time brings better results. To put it another way, a good friend is more likely to come to your aid than a stranger suddenly beseeched for help. Below is a table of correspondences with suggested offerings and altar items.

Planet	Colour	Metal and precious items	Influences	Altar items
Sun	Yellow	Gold, ruby, garnet, & other red stones	Vitality, visibility & recognition	Business card, an award, photo of yourself
Moon	White	Silver, pearl, moonstone, clear quartz seashells & water	Unconscious, family, belonging	Family photos, kids' drawings, your dream journal, mirrors
Mercury	Multi-coloured	Quicksilver; opal, agate, gems with variegated colours	Communication, education & travel	Your car keys, a notebook, your phone
Venus	Green (and pink)	Copper, diamond & other white gems	Love, attraction, pleasure	Perfume, beautiful items, jewellery, fragrant flowers, sweet foods
Mars	Red	Iron, coral, carnelian, red jasper	Courage, aggression, defence	Gym membership, spicy foods, sharp items, your athame
Jupiter	Royal purple with yellow	Tin, yellow sapphire, citrine & other yellow gems	Knowledge, luck & generosity	A lottery ticket, donations to charity, luxury items, your BoS
Saturn	Black	Lead, obsidian, onyx & other dark crystals	Long-term goals, bindings & endings	Bones, dried leaves, old/inherited items, leather.

Planetary days and hours

Each day of the week is associated with a planet and deity. Planetary days are a fantastic way to introduce a regular spiritual practice to your day (or night), make offerings to the planet/God of the day.

Planetary hours are not the same as clock hours, because a planetary 'day' begins at sunrise and ends at sunset. The time between sunrise and sunset is then divided into 12 to calculate the planetary hours. This means that the planetary 'hours' during the day in Summer will be longer than the planetary hours of a Summer's night, and vice versa in Winter. At the equinoxes, the planetary hours during both day and night are close to an even 60 mins.

Day of the Week	Day Ruler	Night Ruler
Sunday	Sun	Jupiter
Monday	Moon	Venus
Tuesday	Mars	Saturn
Wednesday	Mercury	Sun
Thursday	Jupiter	Moon
Friday	Venus	Mars
Saturday	Saturn	Mercury

Each planetary hour is ruled by a planet, according to the Chaldean order: Saturn, Jupiter, Mars, Sun, Venus, Mercury, Moon. The planets of Uranus, Neptune, and Pluto don't rule a day or an hour, because the ancient astrologer-astronomers could not see them in the sky; they were invisible until telescopes were invented.

Technology is indeed a wonderful thing and there are many websites and apps that will precisely calculate the planetary hours for your location. You don't even need to do that though, because the first planetary hour of the day belongs to the day ruler and the first planetary hour of the night belongs to the night ruler. Just find out what time sunrise and sunset is in your location and you are all set for some planetary magic.

> I avoid magick around eclipses. Eclipses are incredibly unpredictable. Spellwork at this time is like trying to bottle a dragon: the dragon won't like it. At best, you'll waste your effort; at worst, your magick will backfire on you.
>
> Use eclipse season for purification and cleansing practices instead. It's a great time to take a break from pushing your will out into the Universe and cultivate receptivity to what the Universe offers to you.

Bringing Magick into Everyday Life

By Scarlet Paige

How can we integrate magick and ritual into our daily lives? Life itself is a ritual, and it is likely that you participate in hundreds of small rituals every day without even being aware of it. Rituals have been performed by humans for thousands of years. The act of lighting a fire and dancing under a full moon is a ritual that has survived the passing of time. But other rituals can be done by anyone, anywhere and at any time.

You wake, perhaps to an alarm or maybe to your own body clock and greet the day. Sitting up, you stretch, reminding yourself to be thankful for all the positive things in your life. After sliding out of bed, you go to the bathroom to take a shower as you consider your day and the tasks needed. Let the water run over your body as you visualise your mind being strong and resilient.

Sing or chant a mantra or affirmation to help prepare you for the day:
"*I welcome this glorious day and all it brings.*"

Taking a handful of salt. you begin to rub it onto your body saying:
"*I release all negativity and what holds me back from being the best version of myself.*"

Once you feel calm, you leave the shower. You're fully awake as you dry yourself and choose clothes carefully, to suit your mood. You go into the kitchen and have a healthy breakfast, a cup of juice or your favourite beverage. Because you are mindful of what you do, your keys or bike lock are easily found where you put them the night before.

You continue to run affirmations in your head or aloud:
"*I am enough, I am in control of my actions and reactions.*"

These simple, everyday movements and activities are in themselves rituals that we use to calm and orient ourselves to our world. With a little bit of thought and dedication, these types of actions can become infused with magical intent and enhance your life. Let us look at other small steps that can easily turn common actions into meaningful rituals.

Connecting to nature

I sit on a large white sandstone block under a lovely old tree. As I lean back and look up into the foliage, I can see the leaves dancing on the wind. The bright sun is warm on my face and I hear birds sing sweet songs as they shelter on the branches above.

There is magick all around you, but you must stop and pay attention, or you will pass it by without ever knowing it was there. In our everchanging world, everything seems to move at a breakneck pace. We all have somewhere to be, and even when we get there, are we really present? Most of us are already thinking about the next destination, the next event.

Over generations, we have become separated and disengaged from our Mother Earth and Her power. For many of us, the changing of the seasons no longer seems to matter as it once did. We no longer follow the rise and fall of the sun, or the waxing and waning of the moon. Most of us are no longer engaged with the land because we are no longer directly reliant upon it. For those living in a city, links with the land, planting, growing, and harvesting food and tending to animals have been significantly weakened.

Reconnect with Mother Earth and combine the mundane and the magical together to create a collage of practice which will enhance your life. The following daily practices are simple to create, complete and maintain. They will allow you to build upon your own experiences, enhance and direct your own personal power, and bring positive things into your life. It is time to slow down, focus and pay attention.

Scent and smells

Why are certain smells so powerful? Why are they able to transport us back in time or to the place where we first encountered them? Our olfactory system is in the same part of our brain that affects emotions, memory, and creativity. Scents can be excellent for manifesting positive energy and evoking memories and can be used to reset yourself to a specific feeling.

Use essential oils, perfumes, incenses, and balms to enhance your magical and daily practices. Different scents have different effects and a scent that one person finds relaxing can annoy another (or cause an asthma attack) so take time when choosing the right one for you.

Using incense during magical workings or meditation will assist you to attune and easily enter the desired consciousness state. Once you begin to associate a particular smell with a particular activity you will find it becomes easier to get into the right frame of mind for that specific task. I personally use one type of incense to centre myself before a ritual and another when I want to relax or fall asleep. Balms are particularly useful to reduce anxiety levels and calm the mind.

The suggestions in other chapters will get you started; however, due to the complexity and infinite number of variations, you'll need to do further research if you require a scent for a specific purpose. Over time choosing the right scent will become second nature to you.

Everyday environments
Did you know that the average person spends up to one third of their life at work? It's good for our mental and physical health if we can enjoy our work environment. If you are lucky enough to work in a job you like, and have a clean safe environment, you are halfway there. However, if you are struggling at work, there are ways in which you can help improve things so that you find work less boring or limiting. Here are some ideas to make your working environment a happy and more inviting place.

When arriving at work, try to enter your work environment with a happy, cheerful, and positive disposition. Where possible greet co-workers with a smile. Have you ever noticed how many people do not smile and seem so preoccupied with their own day or thoughts? Many people never even take time to offer a cursory *"Hello."*

Think about this simple saying:
'If you see someone without a smile, give them yours.'

This does not have to be a saccharine drenched greeting, just a simple gesture will do – as a bonus, this improves your day as well. Try to acknowledge the people whose paths you cross, even if it is with just a word or a smile. If you find a particular colleague annoying or draining, try to reduce the time spent with them. Some people are more difficult to be around than others and can deplete your energy.

As a society, our connection to nature and animals has been diminishing as we rely on technology and immerse ourselves in plastic and artificial environments. Some workplaces are allowing employees to have plants and even pets in offices and at workstations. Innovative companies ensure that lunch spaces are fitted out to help relax and calm employees.

It is not unusual to spend a whole day inside an artificial environment and not even touch the Earth. This disconnect can be a drain on our physical bodies and spirits. Try to take brain-breaks every hour to stretch and move about. Wherever possible, take time outside to sit on the grass, smell the air, listen to water, and watch the changing of the colours of the sky and trees. Nature is a great energiser and renews the spirit.

Daily life
You have probably heard this before. People say, *"You just need to be more positive!"* However, at times being positive can be difficult. My preferred advice is to try to find just one good thing, because being totally and continuously positive is not always an option. Once you find just one positive slant, it becomes easier to change your overall focus and see what has happened in new and different ways.

Instead of looking at difficult or challenging events in a negative manner consider any positive potential outcomes, effects and opportunities that flow from it. Many things that initially seem unpleasant can be reframed into a positive, given time and contemplation. You may not see the good when something confronting or unpleasant is occurring – or even just after it has occurred – but with hindsight, it's possible to see a benefit from any event.

When you choose to respond to an event with a positive outlook, you do not allow yourselves to become bogged down in that event. You can accept what has occurred and determine whether you will act to correct it or continue and see what eventuates. By doing this, your ability to be resilient and proactive, instead of reactive, increases. Initially, it may be hard to see difficult situations as good, but with practice it becomes easier.

I am not writing here about catastrophic or significant events such as disastrous bushfires or the death of a loved one. Events such as these are on a different scale, can have devastating impacts and therefore require a different response. In some cases, acknowledging – and working through – a process that includes grief or anger is completely appropriate. Putting on a false 'happy face' or spiritually bypassing distressing emotions is not usually the best response to a deeply felt, tragic event.

Learn to differentiate between small inconveniences and the more serious events in life and act accordingly. If something is a small annoyance, such as coffee spilt on a new shirt, you could choose to take it as a sign that you need to slow down. Perhaps the Universe is stopping you from continuing your journey for a reason? Perhaps if you had continued without this small issue you may have encountered a larger issue? Consider that this mishap may have occurred for a reason. Change your shirt or clean up as best you can and move on without expending unnecessary anger and letting it derail your day.

In today's rushed world, it's easy to raise your voice in frustration, but we must remember that relationships are built on – or destroyed by – these daily small interactions. When you speak to others, try to give them your attention and care. Try to take the time to sit in a quiet place and debrief about your day and listen in response to what others have to say. At mealtimes, you may like to speak about a positive aspect of your day, something you are thankful for, even if most of the day has been total chaos.

Protection guardians, mirrors, spells, and sigils

Your home should be a place of safety and peace, a sanctuary where you go to recharge and relax. Using guardians, protections and enhancements can help you to feel safe and happy. An effective door guardian can prevent negative influences – both spiritual and physical – from entering your space and encourage positive influences to manifest. Let's explore some easy options, regardless of whether you own, rent or live with others.

Mirrors have been used for centuries in magick and are considered to be portals to and from other worlds and reflectors of energies. In the past when someone died, all mirrors in the home were turned face down or covered with black fabric. This was because it was believed that the soul of the departed could become trapped in the mirror or become lost on their journey to the Summerlands (or Heaven).

After your home has been cleansed, place a small mirror opposite each door to outside to maintain positive energies inside the dwelling. To ensure these guardian mirrors are not used as portals for negative influences to enter your home, place a protective symbol on the back of mirrors to block them as an entry point. If you are using a separate mirror in your magical workings, wrap in a black cloth when not in use and place a crystal with it.

Creating a guardian is useful way to define a point of protection for a building, yard or enclosure. These guardians can take many forms and are easily hidden if you wish to do so. A small totem of any kind can be used, such as a ceramic face, a crystal, or any item you can imbibe with your power and need. Place these items practically anywhere inside or outside the home, car or even at work.

No matter where I live, I put a crystal in each corner of the yard, as well as at any gate that could be considered an entrance. These crystals should be chosen with specific intent. If you are not sure which crystals to use, then the most useful crystal for this is clear quartz.

These do not need to be large specimens and may be tumbled stones or crystal shards. Place one in each of the four corners of your yard or home. Alternatively, you could place the crystals in the four cardinal directions (North, South, East and West) using a compass for accuracy.

It is best to place crystals on a Full Moon, while walking clockwise around the property. At each point ask a guardian or the Gods to protect you, your home and all those in it. As you walk about your boundary visualise white light forming a protective dome over your entire space. For more information about specific crystals, please see the chapter *Crystals and Earth Magick*.

I have small plaster casts or faces representing the Goddess above each of my doors. These faces have been consecrated with essential oils, tasked with protecting my home and are hidden in plain sight.

If you prefer to use a written form of protection, then use a symbol or sigil to help manifest your desires. A sigil (a magical picture, symbol or diagram) can be as large or small as you wish to suit a position or area. They can be placed in an obvious location or tucked away in places such as under the welcome mat or the letterbox. They can be drawn on any piece of paper or even on windows/glass. A sigil can also be created and carried on your person, in a wallet or placed in your car. There are many ways to create personalised and potent sigils and, if this idea appeals, I encourage you to explore further.

Items of power

Witches know items hold the resonance of those who use and own them. Even the smallest items, such as a pendant, ring, comb, or teacup, hold the essence and power of its wearer/owner. That resonance or essence may last long after the original owner is gone. Maybe you have a special dress or pair of shoes that you feel are lucky and bring you good fortune when worn. Perhaps you have a necklace or ring you wear on special occasions. Items worn every day and over time collect the essence of their owner, become attuned to them, and thus become an item of power.

The simple act of getting dressed each day is an opportunity to choose items of clothing or jewellery for confidence or calm or ancestral strength (or any other intention). I have ritual jewellery I wear when working magick, meditating, or during ritual.

You may be lucky enough to have an item that has been passed down through the generations to you from a relative, and feel it holds special power. These items can allow you to connect with your ancestor/s when worn. Items which have been worn for a long time, such as engagement, wedding or eternity rings can have deep emotional bonds with their owner. You may like to carefully consider who you wish your own special items to go to after you die.

New ritual jewellery can be chosen with specific purposes in mind and should be cleansed and consecrated before being worn in circle. See the *Consecration Ritual* chapter for more information about how to prepare an item for magical working. If you purchase a pre-loved item, you will want to cleanse it before use as well. To ensure magical items attract only positive energies, cleanse regularly by methods such as bathing in rainwater or place in the Full Moon light overnight. It is also useful to wrap them in a dark cloth with a clear quartz crystal to help nurture them.

Years ago, I recall being given a beautiful, antique silver ring with a large burgundy garnet set on top. This vintage piece was stunning to look at, but once I took it out of the box and touched it, I felt uncomfortable, as if my fingers were somehow dirty. I cleansed the ring in rainwater and in moonlight, and even went so far as to wrap it in a cloth and bury it in the garden for seven days on a waning Moon. No matter what I did I felt that I could not remove the 'negative essence' of the previous wearer. I had other people try on the ring, and most of them also felt unsettled. I decided the ring was not for me, but I could not, in good conscience, bring myself to give it away or sell it. So, to this day it sits in the box unworn. Maybe over years, the essence of the ring will diminish, but only time will tell.

Travel magick

I love to travel. I love the idea of travel. I like going to new and exciting places. However, when I travel, I always have two things on my mind:
1. Will the plane fall out of the sky?
2. Will my luggage make it to my destination?

A long time ago, a good friend told me that carrying a small totem of a pig in my luggage would be lucky and ensure both myself and my luggage would arrive safely. Ever since that time, I have carried two small pig items, one in my carry-on bag and one in my checked luggage.

So why a pig? (I can almost hear you asking me that question.) Pigs have always been considered fortunate, and a symbol of abundance. The more pigs you possessed, the wealthier you were. They were used for various purposes including meat and trade. In some cultures, the gift of a pig in dowries was a sign of the family's wealth.

Whenever I travel, I bring two small pig figurines with me. I acquired my two lucky travel pigs at a two-dollar shop back in the 1980s. They are made of some sort of plaster or resin and have been painted gold. They are the size of a small matchbox and pop easily into the small spaces in my bags. These simple items have kept my bags, the contents and me safe for years. Surprisingly enough, travel pigs can be easily found in many places and do not have to be expensive or precious. If you cannot find one in a discount shop, then you can use any small pig token such as the plastic pigs you find in a farmyard toy set.

When I know I am going to travel for any extended time, I make time to anoint both pigs and reconsecrate them with their tasks in mind. I imbue them with my intent, using an essential oil and consecrate them with a simple action phrase such as:

"Token of luck used for travel, never let my luck unravel,
Keep safe all that is with me, as I do will, so mote it be."

When I am feeling anxious about travelling and especially when going on a road trip, I carry a small white, cotton bag filled with a red jasper, basil, mugwort, rosemary, and some protection oil I mixed up. Sometimes I add a piece of purple cord tied with the number of knots for the days or hours I will be away. For example, if my trip will last two weeks, then I tie 14 knots in the cord. I keep this in my car, or in my hand luggage or bag. I refresh this bag every six months or so, or just before a big trip. The pigs are better for international travel, but I prefer this small spell bag for local trips.

Do not use a spell bag when travelling overseas, as the herbs in the bag may appear to be illegal. Be aware that some fruit, bark, leaves or seeds are prohibited from being taken across some state borders in Australia.

You are better off choosing a crystal or travel pig for international trips.

Crystals

When buying a crystal, ask the seller about the origin of the crystal and if it has been ethically sourced. Some distributors use dyed crystals and try to fake more expensive specimens. If you need semi-precious stones or crystals in spellwork or spell bags, you might like to use small, more economically priced, tumbled stones. Picking up an unusual rock from the roadside or beach (not a National Park!) is another alternative. Hag stones (rocks with a naturally formed hole all the way through) are particularly magical.

There are many uses for crystals. They can be used when meditating, exercising, or sleeping. Try placing one in each palm when meditating. You may like to buy a crystal cradle or make one from string. This will enable you to swap and change the crystal you use to suit your needs. You wear the cradle around your neck as a pendant. I have also been known to tuck a crystal in my bra or pocket.

You can use crystals to make your home or workspace more harmonious. If you use a computer all day long, place a large chunk of clear crystal next to your computer to help balance energies. Many people also use rock salt lamps to help cleanse the air in their home and workspaces of negative ions. I enjoy the soft light that salt lamps cast, but you must regularly check the light fitting and metal frame that holds it, as the salt will corrode the metal parts quickly.

Conscious consumption

Even simple tasks such as shopping and eating can become mindful, positive ritualised experiences. When shopping for supplies, consider the effect your purchases might have. Try and choose products that have been ethically sourced and grown. If you eat meat, consider its origin and how it has been farmed. Some choose to take this further and adopt vegetarian or vegan food choices to avoid cruel animal farming practices. Whatever you choose, do your best to live in harmony with your environment.

When buying clothes or shoes, ask or research the origin of products. For example, does the company producing the item have sustainable and ethical practices? Subscribe to fair trade practices, which are part of the changing face of brands helping emerging countries and their people to earn a decent wage. These brands may be a bit more expensive and a little harder to source, but you will have the satisfaction of knowing you are not promoting or contributing to the sadness and pain of others.

When shopping use sustainable packaging, including fruit bags and fabric shopping bags. Carry a reusable fabric bag so that you can say "no" to plastic. In the kitchen, choose to use beeswax wraps or ecofriendly containers when storing produce or leftovers.

Gardening can be part of your environmentally sustainable efforts. The actions of gardening and then using vegetables that you have grown yourself are relaxing and almost meditative processes. By spending time in your garden, you align yourself with nature and feel the turning of the Wheel of the Year as it moves through the seasons. When growing produce, you will be able to see the circle of life from seedling to fruit to seed. There is a great deal of satisfaction in eating something you have grown from a seedling and harvested yourself. You can also start a worm farm to compost food scraps. These practices align us with the Earth and remind us of simpler times.

You may like to look into minimalism to purchase and contribute less to the over-production of useless items that are choking our world. Consumerism can be seen as the latest in a long line of dependencies and addictions today. The idea of amassing large quantities of material items in the hope of finding happiness is like trying to fill a hole that has no bottom. The more you buy, the more you want. Why do we buy so many useless items?

People purchase material things for a variety of reasons that include:
- compensating for something
- as a sign of success
- wanting to hide behind possessions
- wanting to impress others
- jealousy of what others have.

In Australia, we are fortunate to have publicly funded healthcare and benefits. While there are inequities, and some people live below the poverty line, overall our country experiences a high level of affluence.

When some people lose the connection to the things that really matter, such as healthy relationships, communities, and their sense of self-worth, they may try to find a way to fill this loss. You do not actually require that much to survive and still enjoy life. You need food, water, and shelter, as well as human connection. Of course, it is lovely to have a brand new car to drive and own an expensive home but when does it become too much? When do possessions begin to own us instead of us owning them? The more some people have, the more they seem to desire. If everyone decided they did not need new items to replace items that are still usable, we would see a stunning change in society.

Try to invest in experiences instead of buying new items that are not necessary. Take a trip to a beautiful location and share the views. Give your time and resources to those who have less wealth or privilege than you do. Go walking or hiking and spend time talking to one another. When we are not surrounded by clutter and things, we have more time to focus on things that matter. You oversee your future, and only you can change your moral and ethical compass.

A Witch's Apothecary

By Ki-ian

> 'The earth is our mother, we sing.
> Mother earth, mother nature – she is the literal womb of life, providing all that we need. Her living soil feeds us; her rocks make our bones; her minerals are in our life's blood. The very heart of Goddess spirituality and of other indigenous traditions is the recognition that the earth is sacred.'
> Starhawk in *The Earth Path: Grounding Your Spirit in the Rhythms of Nature* (page 158).

Welcome to the witch's apothecary. A place where I take you for a walk down one of the witch's many pathways, sharing knowledge about herbs and their correspondences, uses, spells and potions. There is *so* much to talk about. Before I get into all the goodness of working with herbs and conjuring, you must understand your relationship to the plant world and remember your connection to nature as witch.

A witch embodies matter. Growing, wildcrafting and making. You are the conjuror, the spell worker who enables magick to flow from soil to soul. A witch's apothecary is a place where the beauty of these ingredients (soil, plant, organic matter, active constituents, volatile oils, energy, cellulose and fibre) are invited to alchemise into magick and support spellwork and healing.

In the apothecary, it is the plant's opportunity to have their moment. To shine. You are here to guide, channel (and sometimes do as you're told) supporting the plant magick to reach its potential and grace.

Working with herbs the witch's way enhances the work (spells, meditations, rituals) and enables us to make devotional offerings, set intention and add substance to the energy of witchcraft.

You *are* nature and by understanding your place in this amazing ecosystem (with help from a small balcony garden with a cityscape backdrop to a herbal apothecary set on rolling acres) you have the opportunity to access a web of information and magick like no other. My hope is that this chapter will introduce you to the basics and from there you will fly beyond the rules and correspondences into a world of discovery of communication and connection with the world of our magical plants.

Whether your journey takes you down a pathway of kitchen witching, blending and mixing brews, or to become a master of baneful herbs and potions, I hope you enjoy this chapter as you take your first steps into your own witch's apothecary.

How do modern witches gather herbs today? To use herbs in magical practice, you begin by listening to the cadence of the earth. This starts with breathwork, meditation and commitment to understanding the cycles and how these relate to working magick and herbs.

Herb correspondences

Moon stage	Garden	Essence	Plant stage
Waning / dark moon	Mulch /compost	Surrender / deep stillness	Soil / roots
New moon	Prepare /feed	Vibrating / begin	Seed
Half moon	Intention / harvest	Flow / potential	Bud / flower
Full moon	Harvest/ gratitude	Release / surrender	Harvest

Aligning the use of the herbs with each of these stages adds potency whilst casting magick. For example, if you are conjuring a working to help you with a decision and you need to sit with all the factors of your potential situation, you may need the essence of stillness. A working for this time may be done over the waning/dark moon stage to support clarity within the stillness of the earth and moon cycle, using herbs that support introspection.

Another example is if you were looking to grow something new, such as start a venture or secure a job. Conjure at the time of the new moon with herbs and seeds that align with your spell's intent.

Each moment of the earth's cadence and moon cycle gives you an opportunity to enhance your magic and workings. You do this by aligning yourself and your practice into their rhythm. When you flavour your spellwork and rituals with herbs, you enhance your focus and intent, your purpose.

Conjuring with consciousness – regenerative magick

Working with herbs to heal and enhance magick – whether it be in the form of carrying *Ruta graveolens* (rue) in your pocket for protection or slipping a little

Artemesia vulgaris (mugwort) under your pillow to support lucid dreaming – has been happening since time began from the witch in the woods until now. Today, almost every herb is available to be purchased anywhere in the world with little more than a click. Yet it would be remiss of me not to introduce you to the world of regenerative magick and invite you to embody your eco-responsibility.

The first opportunity when conjuring with consciousness is to understand that the plants we work with as witches can both harm and heal. Plants are the original medicine and as such should be approached with respect, knowledge and a healthy dose of research. One example is beloved rue (*Ruta graveolens*) which is contraindicated in pregnancy. Knowing our plant constituents, uses and warnings not only ensures that what we use is fit for purpose, it also makes sure we are safe. Learning herbal monographs is an imperative part of working with plants as our allies in casting. Links to free monograph sites have been added in the back of this book to support your learning.

It's imperative that you, as a modern-day witch, learn to conjure with consciousness and understand where and how your magical herbs and/or essential oils have been grown and harvested. Were the farming practices regenerative for the earth? Who grew the herbs? How were they produced? Were the harvest workers paid a fair wage? How were they harvested? These are great questions to ask your suppliers, with the answers not only improving the integrity of your magical working, but also the ecology of the earth, whose pulse enhances your magick with every step.

I remember the first thing I learnt wildcrafting, so many years ago, was to not harvest from a roadside as the carbon monoxide from car emissions are found in the harvested matter, as well as more obvious concern of road safety.

Some of the herbs that we learn to use in our blends and brews may be considered noxious weeds in parts of Australia. By knowing your plant identifications and ensuring your harvesting techniques don't spread seed or harm (do no harm in all things), you're ensuring the integrity of your magic.

Whether wildcrafting or purchasing, growing or community sharing, it makes sense to question the origin of your magical tools, with herbs being no exception. Or better still, begin your own magical herb garden.

Your witch's garden

There is no better way to understand the potential for plant magick than to grow a plant from seed, observing all its stages of growth. Growing, harvesting and working with plants embodies the magical energy that emanates within our spellwork. With a basic understanding of how things are grown and fully immersing yourself in the spirit of the plants, you will come to understand the entirety of their offerings.

Before a seed sprouts, there is a moment when the seed vibrates, just as the sprout breaks the shell's surface. When you think about this in practical terms, you are able to provide the right environment to support the seeds to grow. You understand the importance of keeping the soil moist, the quality of the water provided, positioning the plants and how you support them to capture the sun. Immerse yourself in all aspects of your witch's garden, whether it be in your own backyard, on a balcony or benchtop or a shared space within your local community garden. It's here that the magick truly begins.

Your outer landscape
Embodying your surrounding landscape, identifying the plant beings around you and sitting in nature observing the interactions – from the smallest of creatures traversing the soil to the birds in the sky – is all a part of the green witch's world. By acknowledging and understanding the land upon which you live, you take the first steps of enhancing your journey into green witchcraft.

Coming to understand the country that surrounds you can be done in so many ways. You can observe the prevailing winds, how the sun moves through the seasons, where excess water flows and pools after heavy rain. You can feel how the soil meets your feet as you take a step. Knowing your outer landscape and how it in turn witnesses you, you are able to integrate any kind of witch's apothecary garden into your own local ecology with minimal disturbance. All the time harvesting sunshine, water and nutritional resources with efficiency and flow.

Soil
Building your soil (if you don't already have a garden accessible) is possibly one of the most important things you'll do. Soil is the foundation of nutrition in which your herbs and their magic will grow. There is so much information available to help you build a small or large garden, depending on your space and time, so I won't go deeply into it in this chapter. I've included a few resources at the end of this text and the concepts from these can be applied absolutely anywhere.

Compost and balance of organic matter, nutrients and moisture are key. Permaculture practices and principles will set you off on the right path and will teach aspecting, bioregional planting guidance, observation and practical setup of your magical garden. The main thing you need to know is that it can be done anywhere. You can have two pots on a windowsill, a greenhouse in a city backyard, or rolling acres of gardens. Your intent is to build relationships with the herbs you are growing, enhancing your magick and charging your spellwork with an energy like no other.

Plant communication

My mentor in plant communication, Cathy Skipper, has a saying that completely changed how I communicate with any plant matter. It is: *'I touch and I am touched'*. This is a phrase that, when consciously connecting with plants, I repeat over and over until I receive a response. These words open our human minds and hearts to the potential that plants are vibrational matter and can respond to us when reached out to. Think about it for a moment: *plants are vibrational matter and can respond to us when reached out to.*

How does this change how you grow, care for, cultivate and use your magical herbs within your practice? In your witch's apothecary, the potency of herbs is increased pending the conversations had with each of them. Stillness, breathwork and opening the heart are three simple pathways to such communication. A simple way of communicating is to sit in the same place, whether it be in front of the potted mugwort on your balcony or under the wizened branches of the sheoak in the botanic gardens, in stillness. Breathe deeply, exchange with the tree carbon dioxide and oxygen, and slowly open your heart to the rhythm and energy of the plant you're connecting with. Remain focused only on the plant. Breathe deeply. Listen. It is during these moments of plant communication that I have received great clarity and insight.

Herbs

The invitation for both the novice or experienced witch is to honour the cadence of nature and *go slow*. Setting yourself up for success means sometimes choosing to grow a smaller range of plants. Think about the correspondence table and choose one or two herbs that resonate with you. Research, and if you're an absolute beginner who feels that you're not able to grow anything, ensure your choice of herbal magick is one of the simpler herbs to grow. There is magick in all plants.

Corn has powers of protection and luck (and is really simple to grow) and coriander is a wonder in love spells. Want to get to the root of a matter? Comfrey is your companion here. Looking to work with fertility, health and wisdom? The humble sunflower is your ally. A truly giving herb, they'll grow anywhere and provide an abundance of magick and joy (and an opportunity to save seeds).

After the herbs are chosen and grown, you can begin to think about harvest. This is an important process in building the energy of magick wherein our focus and intent once again become important. Before harvesting your herbs, take a moment. A moment to breathe, honour and give thanks to the plant. I like to tell plants what I am doing with them. This can be many different conversations; however, it usually goes down something like this: "*Morning Rosemary, I'm here today to harvest you. I'll be distilling you for essential oils. Deepest of gratitude for growing so beautifully through all we have been through together since the last harvest.*" It's here I stop and listen.

I make an offering to the plant and begin the harvest. In my own garden or when wildcrafting I make an offering every time I harvest. My wildcrafting bag has a pouch filled with lovingly stored crystals, beads, feathers and hair (yes, hair) that I offer in gratitude for the harvest. On my home garden and farm, my offering is usually in the form of a prayer or moment of silence and gratitude.

At this point, you have completely honoured the plant for their contribution to your magick. You've acknowledged the constant exchange of biology and sugars that has been happening deep under the soil since the seed first vibrated into sprout. You've offered your own breath and heart over to the plant including the wisdom held within the phytochemicals and constituents that flow through the plant. You're honouring the very chemistry that makes this plant what it is. This acknowledgment deeply enhances your magick.

Apothecary basics

Your witch's apothecary can be set up wherever suits your budget, space and time. The most amazing setups I have seen are mobile and elegantly simple. A backpack with a boline, altar cloth and muslin, some small jars and a pinch of salt is just as efficient to brew magic as a fully established apothecary with all the trimmings. Personally, I love to scour second-hand shops for my bowls, jugs, jars etc. There are no rules in terms of what you should or should not have in your apothecary except 'do no harm', which also means to yourself. My personal practice is that all ritual tools and things genuinely needed to get the job done will arrive as and when I need them. Common sense prevails when taking herbs from matter through to magick and these workings come with a general overarching 'don't leave a lit candle unattended' waiver.

Here's a list of general tools that will support you as you begin:

- ✦ ***A good knife/boline.*** I have specific knives for magick and kitchen work. Keep your edges sharp and ready.
- ✦ ***Cutting board.*** As we're just using organic matter, wooden boards will do. Remember to keep them clean and oil regularly.
- ✦ ***Glass jug and assorted bowls.*** Fantastic for mixing and brewing. I have ritual bowls and mixing bowls. Saucers and jar lids also suffice.
- ✦ ***Measuring cups and spoon measures.***
- ✦ ***Sieve.***
- ✦ ***Herb grinder.*** Manual or electric.
- ✦ ***Recycled jars, old essential oil bottles and masking tape for labels.*** Labelling of all prepared herb matter is essential. Trust me (smile). You think you'll remember but you won't!
- ✦ ***Salt.*** Good quality salt belongs in every magical working.
- ✦ ***Mortar and pestle.*** These are easy to find online, in second-hand shops and, of course, in all good kitchen shops.
- ✦ ***Drying racks/harvest baskets.*** Oven racks work nicely, and food dryers work a treat.
- ✦ ***An offering for exchange when harvesting.*** See 'Herbs' section.

Don't forget the most important tool in your apothecary and when working with herb magick is you – yes, you! The magick begins and ends with you. The more vibrant your body and connection to matter are, the stronger the workings.

Brewing it all together

Magick is the art of changing consciousness at will (according to Dion Fortune), and our herbal allies are one of the conduits to manifestation, directing the current on a pathway of focus and intent.

In your novice journey through this chapter, you've acknowledged the landscape, worked your soil, chosen your herbs and grown, harvested and stored your magical herbs. Now for the final brew, where magick and matter merge together. I will share some workings that hopefully show you how this all comes together to strengthen your rituals.

One of my favourite Tarot decks is the Mary El Tarot. In the book accompanying the cards, Mary El talks about following magic through. She shares a Hebrew quote that has never left me: *'Pray for God and row for the shore'*.

Such wisdom in these words. We, as witches working with herbs to enhance our magic, are engaged in both the prayer and the rowing. The prayer is the plant communication. The prayer is following the cadence of the earth. The rowing is the hands working the soil. The rowing is the harvesting, storing and working with plant matter to make magick.

As in any ritual, when preparing spellwork with herb magick it is important to have everything prepared and in front of you ready to go. Here I share some brews developed for ritual with The Circle Coven and also recipes from my personal practice. Whether these spells are made in your coven or by you alone, being prepared with all the ingredients is a 'ritual hack' that ensures the energetic flow of the working. It's also a part of honouring yourself, the plants and your coven members. Remember, potentially, you've grown some of these ingredients from seed; at the very least, you know where they have come from. Maybe you've harvested, dried, and cared for them. Finish the energetic work by preparing your ritual mindfully and with reverence to all the energies that have brought you to this place.

This is only the beginning of your journey into the world of enhancing your practice with herbs. Remember to have fun! Enjoy these spellwork recipes. Simple in their ingredients, they pack a punch in terms of potential and energy.

Vitality oil
Ground – Love – Regenerate

You will need:
- 25 ml empty glass bottle
- Apricot kernel oil
- Essential oils of sandalwood, rose and grapefruit
- Dried rose petals.

Focus:
Within you there is a connection to life force. This connection is strengthened by what you add to your physical, emotional and spiritual self. You choose what you allow in, what you add and how you brew your own vitality.

Your vitality can be influenced by many things such as nutrition, dance, emotions, love, desire, play, art, laughter or fear.

The nutrient rich apricot kernel oil represents your blood. The carrier of nutrients around your body. The very nature of matter within yourself.

The glass bottle in this working represents your physical self. Forged from the earth, you are strong, resilient, fragile and delicate.

The rose represents your spirit. Love is the Law. Love is the Bond.

Essential oil of sandalwood represents strength and supports groundedness in all things. Rose opens the heart and invites you to live to your full potential. Grapefruit emotionally purifies and releases.

Craft:
On the full moon, set your circle, cast your quarters and light your candle. The veil envelopes you in your ritual and you begin. You are conscious of each ingredient and what it offers the blend. Charging your glass bottle between your palms, first add the dried rose petals. This is your spirit. This is love.

Breathe.

Pour in your base oil until it fills to the bottom of the neck of the bottle. This is your blood.

Breathe.

Add five drops of sandalwood essential oil– strength and grounding.

Breathe.

Add three drops of rose essential oil to open your heart and live.

Breathe.

Add two drops of grapefruit essential oil to purify and release.

Tighten the lid on the bottle and begin to shake the brew chanting:
  "Full moon vitality come into me, as I do will so it shall be."

Raise the energy as you repeat this verse over and over. Use body percussion, movement, rhythm and flow to charge your brew.

Allow the brew to sit under the full moon. You now have 'Vitality Oil'. This can be decanted into a roller and taken with you every day for use when you need a lift. It is also an energetic and positive ritual anointing oil.

Persephone loose incense

I love making incense and, in particular, for ritual a loose incense is just delicious. The smoke is heady and clears the energies of the room. This blend was made as I began a journey with Persephone whilst planting out pomegranate trees on our farm. I had the ingredients on hand and felt the roots, woods and resins held the frequency of descent, with the rose petals resonating a return to heart.

You will need:
- 1 part palo santo
- 1 part Australian sandalwood
- 1 part vetiver root
- 2 parts dark frankincense resin
- 1 part ground rose petals
- A pinch of dried rose petals (whole).

With your mortar and pestle, grind the frankincense. Add the Australian sandalwood, palo santo and chopped vetiver root and, finally, the ground rose petals. Add the whole petals and place in a sealed container to store.

I use bamboo charcoal disks that have little or no chemical in them, thus making them environmentally friendlier to burn loose incense on.

Ritual body scrub

How do you prepare for ritual? One of my favourite things to do before ceremony is to fast and bathe. This ritual body scrub recipe is perfect preparation for entering sacred space, connecting with the divine and conjuring magick.

The scrub should be brewed mindfully.

You will need:
- 1 part pink sea salt
- ½ part pink clay (white clay works beautifully well too)
- Body oil of choice (I use apricot kernel oil)
- Dried calendula flower petals
- Dried rose petals
- 3 drops frankincense essential oil
- 1 drop lemon tea tree essential oil.

Blend the sea salt, dried flowers and clay in a clean bowl. In another bowl, add the essential oils to the body oil, then gradually moisten the dry ingredients with the combined oils until they form a ball when gathered. Place into a sealed jar and keep in a cool place.

Rinse your body mindfully. Take care as you run your hands over your skin. What are you thinking? Where is your focus and intent? Prepare your body for ritual in your own way. Stepping away from the shower, take a deep breath and connect. Connect with your ritual intent and allow your mind to clear as you take a small amount of scrub in each hand and slowly begin to cleanse your skin in circular motions.

Rinse well. Repeat if you wish.

Resources and references for this chapter

Solum Farm. Request access to our online store to dive into workshops, learn about collaboration opportunities and buy herbs grown from seed to soul. <www.solumfarm.com/witchesapothecary>

Rosemary Morrow *Earth Users Guide to Permaculture*. <www.store.holmgren.com.au/product/earth-users-guide-to-permaculture>

Crystals and Earth Magic

By Jacq Hackett

I remember when I was a young child in England. I used to go out to collect wild blackberries with my grandmother and return home with my hands and face stained purple, my hair full of flowers or feathers and my pockets full of rocks and stones. Although my foraging adventures began almost fifty years ago, I distinctly remember ambling carefree through the countryside with my nostrils full of earthy scents and a basket too big for a three-year-old to carry. Needless to say, I often spent more time dawdling in a world of my own.

If it wasn't the forest fruits I shoved into my mouth or ornamental garlands I (with likewise grace) shoved into my hair, it was the call of the crystals I found along the way that stopped me in my tracks. Long after the few surviving blackberries were baked into pies and eaten, the flowers pressed or made into essences, the feathers trimmed and dipped into inkwells for sketching, only the rocks remained. Polished and gleaming, the stones would jingle and chatter in my pockets and I found my fingers would often seek them out to connect and reassure them that I was listening and hadn't forgotten them.

Rocks and crystals continued to catch my attention throughout adulthood. I even married into a mining family who ran a rock gallery on a large estate in the Kimberley. My daughters have likewise been surrounded by rocks, crystals and precious stones all their formative years. As young women, they have rock collections that even I envy! Now, as a mature woman in my fifties, I still enjoy foraging in my own garden and taking long walks through forest trails. Every now and then a stray crystal or rock will catch my attention and call out to me... but more often, it is the jingling and chatter of the crystals in my pocket, in my car, or on my windowsill that I talk back to. Just to reassure them I am listening and haven't forgotten them.

How to talk to crystals

Crystals, with their fascinating beauty, have turned children and adults alike into gem enthusiasts the world over. Often, local market stalls and gem shows provide the best introduction into the secret language of crystals. Sometimes, prospective buyers aren't even aware of the communication exchange that is happening. Witches eagerly rummage through boxes and trays of stones to find a special rock needed for a certain spell or magical working, knowing the perfect crystal would jump out, or call out in a way to stand apart from the rest. Seeing, holding and sensing how a crystal and potential owner communicate forms a major part of the selection – it's a two-way conversation – something that should be done in person.

The best market stall keepers are usually lapidary club members or fossickers who can confirm where the crystals were originally located, by whom and how they were mined and the mineral properties they possess. These stones tend to be expensive, but are excellent quality. Some crystal shops and market stalls buy their raw stock from ethically mined sources and pass on the higher expense to cover regular overheads. They can also confirm where, who and how... and the initial meet-and-greet conversation with these stones can still be felt.

Unfortunately, a large number of third-party suppliers have begun selling crystals at markets as beautiful jewellery or loose stones, with limited or zero knowledge of their original source. With the explosive increase in new age advocates of wellness and healing, the demand for crystals has seen competing online stockists lowering the quality of stones and reducing their prices. It is becoming increasingly difficult to know where and under what circumstances these cheaper crystals have been mined. Ethical and sustainable mining is now a grave concern for anyone who can communicate with crystals. The conversation with these stones can feel wrong or faint.

No matter how or where crystals are acquired, they reveal their nature through personal connection, as crystals are so much more than just colourful rocks. The differing shapes, colours and molecular structure of crystals generate unique vibrations., and our own energy centres ('chakras') connect with these vibrations and speak to each other. For example, when crystals are placed on the body or in a crystal healing grid, there is a two-way communication: an absorption of your energy into the crystals, a merging and alteration of vibrational waves as they are reflected and refracted within the crystalline matrices, before a powerful release of focussed energy enters our body, where the process is repeated. It is so important to work with healthy, happy crystals and rocks.

Sometimes a stone or rock will feel wrong to you. Reasons for this can include:

- ✦ The energy is not aligned with how the crystal will be used, for example, using a red oxide stone for the throat chakra.
- ✦ Blockages – especially when sold as one type of crystal but is, in fact, an artificially coloured stone.
- ✦ The crystal has over-absorbed negative energy and needs to be cleansed. This happens more often when purchasing online from unethical mining/supply sources. Try looking for forgotten crystals at garage sales and thrift shops.

Remember to hold each crystal close, listen to its message and sense how this changes your energy, thoughts and feelings. With a basic understanding of how to spot a fake, the sensation of holding a crystal close will reveal much more than an online image. No amount of research can replace the magical connection when two energies merge. Think of the meeting of energies like old friends being reunited – your relationship with a crystal should be similar to your own relationships with people: focus on quality over quantity.

Working with crystals
Understanding the secret language of crystals and their unique vibrations helps witches to redirect energy. Different crystals assist the flow of different energies. Healing with crystals helps rid the body and mind of blockages to improve physical and emotional wellbeing.

New witches often tap intuitively into crystal energy healing when choosing jewellery. You might choose an amethyst ring when you're working with Tarot or psychic abilities, or perhaps you might wear a citrine necklace when going for a job interview. The practical use and knowledge of individual crystal properties helps you to alter a particular state of being or consciousness and focus the energy where it is most beneficial.

The keys to magical workings and self-care include mindfulness, intent and shadow work: identifying what may be missing, repressed or going on within, beneath the conscious ego. From there, with an understanding of how crystals absorb, transform and release energy, you can then choose which crystal is best for the situation. Whether a crystal merely catches your eyes, or you feel a physical pull toward one, your mindful self-investigations will guide you intuitively to the crystal that's right for your purpose.

Charging and cleansing your crystals

Because crystals absorb energies and retain energetic echoes of the people (and events) they have come into contact with, newly acquired crystals and well used favourites need to be cleansed to bring them to a pure and harmonious state.

Before working with any crystal, whether a single stone or within a grid, ensure your chosen crystals are charged and cleansed. Be careful when leaving them out in the sun, or overnight in dew or rain. Some crystals such as rose quartz and amethyst, fade in direct sunlight and lose their beautiful deep colours (although fading will not lessen their unique vibrations). Similarly, porous crystals such as selenite cannot be left out in wet weather or cleansed in water. Here are some options for cleansing and recharging your crystals:

Sun. Strong and direct, the fire energy of the sun sears away old energy from crystals and fills them with light photons (electromagnetic energy). The heat will also transfer into the stone so that it becomes hot to the touch. A partially shaded windowsill or tabletop near the window may be better than the full force of the sun. This method cleanses and recharges all crystals, stones and gems, but will cause deep-coloured, semi-transparent crystals to fade. Be careful to protect amethyst, aquamarine, citrine, fluorite, celestite, kunzite, opal, topaz and rose quartz. Also be aware that direct sunlight through crystals can act as a lens to start fires – so choose your placement carefully.

Moon. The brightest light of the full moon is powerful yet also gentle in its radiation. If you can't place your crystals directly outside under full or waxing moonlight, use a windowsill instead. This method both cleanses and recharges all crystals with soft radiant energy.

Earthing. One of the most natural methods of cleansing and recharging is to place crystals into or onto the earth. Gently resting a crystal on top of a pot plant or covered by the soil allows the earth's own vibrations to recalibrate those within the crystal.

Sound. The vibrations of sound shake up the energy stored within crystals, allowing them to vibrate at a higher frequency. Music, singing, chanting and the ringing of bells permeate the crystalline matrix and 'tune' crystals much like a tuning fork.

Water. Running water and salt water purify crystals by washing out negativity. However, care must be taken when leaving crystals out in rainy weather or leaving for long periods in a bowl or water bottle. The softer, porous crystals (such as selenite, fluorite, gypsum, turquoise and labradorite) will dissolve when they get wet; some leech toxins and poison the water (malachite and pyrite); and mineral-based crystals (hematite and pyrite) will rust and lose their shine. If you are interested in drinking crystal elixirs, it is best to use a bottle that has a separate container for the crystals and not a single chamber for both crystal and water.

Other options. Herb bundles and incense are great options for cleansing all crystals, including porous or light sensitive varieties. Smoke combines Earth, Air and Fire elements and can cleanse a large area. An alternative to smoke is to use selenite's ultra-high frequency to clear and recharge crystals overnight. Selenite is the one crystal that does not require recharging as its iridescent striations continuously refract, giving it the appearance of liquid light. Therefore, it is in a state of constant vibration.

After you've cleansed and charged your crystals and are ready to use them, imprint them by holding them in your hands, closing your eyes, and focussing all of your intention upon them. For instance, if you're planning a crystal working for healing, visualize healing energy filling each of your crystals. You are now ready to begin.

Commonly used crystals

The following is a guide to the common uses of the more popular crystals witches tend to have. Please note the uses suggested in this section do not replace professional medical advice for healthcare conditions.

Clear quartz – the master healer
Clear quartz is one of the most abundant crystals in the world. Its vibrations produce a pure frequency used in modern technology to regulate electrical pulses in radios, watches, satellites and computer chips. This stone is considered the 'perfect jewel' or 'master healer' because it raises the energy level of other crystals, energy sources or body energy centres (chakras) it comes into contact with.

Whilst each chakra is associated with a particular area of the body and a colour of the spectrum, clear quartz can be used for any of the chakra centres for clearing, revitalizing, and healing. Quartz symbolises purity, patience and peace. This is a stone of clarity that amplifies your spiritual antenna and can be used in place of any other crystal. If you have only one crystal in your collection, make it clear quartz.

Rose quartz – universal love
Opening the heart to all types of love (self-love, familiarity, passion and love of life), rose quartz helps to raise self-esteem, restore confidence and balance emotions. It is intricately connected to the heart chakra and is often used to recover from the pain or trauma left from deep emotional wounds. Rose quartz is associated with goddesses of love such as Astarte, Aphrodite and Venus, and can be placed beside the bed to promote harmony and understanding in a relationship. A powerful healing stone that continuously absorbs and alters the energy around it, rose quartz needs to be recharged regularly. Be careful as direct sunlight will cause the beautiful pink colour to fade.

Amethyst – intuition
The gentle vibrations of amethyst help with spiritual practices, specifically deepening the connection to self and intuition. When working toward inner peace, resting and relaxing before sleep, during a stressful situation, or before meditation, amethyst acts as a natural stress reliever that quiets the mind, encourages inner strength and elevates to a higher state of being.

Although not used specifically for protection, by raising the energetic vibration and keeping the spirit at ease, amethyst can be a powerful shield against the distresses or distractions of the outer world. Place in your workspace, in your car or even tucked into clothing to create a more intuitive and peaceful environment. Your energy levels benefit most from a connection with your crystals – whether felt or seen – but at all times close by.

Black obsidian – protection
Black obsidian vibrations create a safe space to develop mental or psychic abilities, communicate with spirit guides and gain insight into the past by opening the mind to higher realms while allowing you to remain grounded and protected. Used as a conduit, black obsidian absorbs negative energies and emotions and focuses them deep into the earth where they can be dispersed and neutralized. This cleared space leaves you free to move through memories and experiences, to gain clarity of current behaviours and foresight into the future. Excellent for shadow work, obsidian helps you unblock your capabilities, strengths and true nature.

Whilst obsidian is prized for dissolving psychic blockages on a metaphysical level, it is equally revered for protection against shock on a cellular level. It is claimed that black obsidian accelerates the healing of wounds, staunches bleeding and reduces the pain of arthritis, joint problems and cramps. Obsidian is also said to improve circulation, warming extremities and lessens hardening of the arteries. This is a particularly useful stone to keep handy in your pocket between Samhain and Yule when the cooler, shorter days lower the immune system.

Onyx – the sorry stone
This stone helps absorb grief, emotional pain and stress. It may calm fears, leading to mental strength and physical self-control. Useful as a course correction, onyx heightens conscious awareness of what you need to do to realign with your higher purpose. To this end, onyx vibrations are beneficial to those undergoing rehabilitation, or needing the strength to change habits and make necessary life changes.

Black stones generally offer protection due to their light absorbing properties. Onyx's greatest value lies in offering support, stability and focus to resolve personal issues and gain perspective unmuddied by sorrow. Use this stone when you need help to begin something new and challenging.

Blue lace agate – serenity
The calming designs of blue lace agate emit soothing vibrations that uplift and elevate the spirit, stimulating a positive effect on emotions and attitude. It is possibly the best crystal to use in times of anxiety and stress due to its gentle encouragement and support. Resonating with the throat chakra, blue lace agate offers confidence and coherence to those who fear public speaking or need to communicate in an intelligent manner, such as teachers, managers or counsellors.

Blue lace agate is said to have properties that reduce pain associated with arthritis and ailments in bone and cartilage – especially within the neck and throat areas. Wearing this beautiful stone around the throat is thought to even assist with balancing weight loss with hypothyroidism and weight gain with hyperthyroidism.

Citrine – luck maker
The vibrant energies of light, happiness and abundance can be felt through citrine. As one of the few crystals that don't hold negative energy, citrine radiates positivity, optimism and financial luck. Because of its association with

the solar plexus chakra, citrine is effective in increasing personal power and self-confidence. A popular gift to newlyweds, newborns, upon graduation or coming of age, citrine brings happiness, confidence, manifestation and wealth.

Citrine is a relatively expensive crystal and highly prized. Beware of fakes. Heat-treated amethyst geodes turn orange but retain the white base and darker tips – an easy spot once you know what you are looking for. Citrine has a consistent colour and occasional horizontal and smooth fault lines – and real crystals never have air bubbles in them!

Garnet – sex
The deep red smouldering fire within garnet connects us to the root chakra to help feel more grounded and connected in the present moment. It also connects to the transformational element of Fire to shatter stagnant energies, giving impetus for change. Exuding healthy sexual vibrations, garnets are associated with increasing creativity, self-expression and confidence – whether in the bedroom or the boardroom, the masculine energy helps to draw on innate, inner strengths and passion.

Lapis lazuli – balance
With its long association with protection, lapis lazuli decorated Tutankhamun's famous golden sarcophagus. Lapis is said to boost a low immune system, lower blood pressure, cleanse organs and reduce the effects of inflammatory diseases. The vibrations of lapis are therefore useful in balancing the body after surgery or healing sprains or pulled muscles.

Lapis lazuli can be beneficial for children and adults who are neurodiverse. Lapis is said to draw awareness to habitual thought patterns and emotions by balancing the brain's right and left hemispheres. It could also be useful for people who suffer from insomnia.

Malachite – transformation
Vibrating with the lush greens of nature, malachite symbolises personal growth, abundance of spirit and treasures of the heart. Being drawn to malachite could mean it is time to prepare for a meaningful but sustainable change by cutting away old belief systems that limit potential.

Technology has provided us with many useful electronic devices that emit harmless electromagnetic protons. However, trouble can arise from overusing these gadgets or living in close proximity to powerlines and radio towers, where heavy, positively charged ions can build up. Malachite may help absorb electromagnetic pollutants from the atmosphere and body and create electrons in the same way as Himalayan salt lamps and copper bracelets work. This polarity charge may increase serotonin levels and bring more oxygen into the blood stream.

Malachite assists in lifting the weight of old traumas or inhibitions and helps develop empathy with others. Draw upon the negatively charged metallic ions in malachite to heal cramps and aid labour, menstrual pain and menopause. Wearing malachite enables you to absorb and process information, break unwanted ties and turn over a new leaf.

Moonstone – destiny
Strongly connected with the waxing and waning feminine energies of the moon, moonstone stimulates the pineal gland and balances hormonal cycles such as puberty, fertility and menopause. This shimmering opaque stone emits receptive vibrations that help soften excessively aggressive energies from an imbalance of estrogen, progesterone or testosterone. By tapping into the body's natural cycles, moonstone can assist with water retention, digestion and other fleshy organs affected by the moon phases.

Moonstone is known to augment psychic predictions by enhancing intuitive perceptions, creative imagination and visualisation. Aligning with the higher forces of the collective consciousness, moonstone connects with the subtle energies of the past to help determine their effect on the present and future. Wear moonstone set in silver when reading Tarot to reveal a clearer destiny.

Selenite – the battery pack
By assisting to remove blockages to create a fluid flow of energy, selenite's vibrations are perfect for cleansing and recharging the spiritual body, energetic spaces and all other crystals. The beautiful striations catch, refract and reflect light in a continuous recharging cycle. This quality allows selenite to provide illumination and purification as it absorbs and dissipates negative energy, replacing it with light and positive energy.

Aligned with the crown chakra, selenite elevates energy, and aligns the self to a higher frequency. By filling our spirit with light, selenite can be used as a protective crystal to shield from malign energy. It is often fashioned into wands for magical use, or towers for recharging a large magical area.

Sodalite – the poet's stone
Thought to conjure profound and poetical discussion on the intricacies of the cosmos, sodalite's patterns strengthen communication, inspiration, and

intuition. In addition to appearing to hold the universe's secrets, sodalite may help you discover the true nature of your own character, challenges and introspections. Sodalite is therefore beneficial in business gatherings such as school or body corporate meetings, where collaboration is needed to promote a unified vision, purpose or goal.

Sunstone – Ra
Carrying the bright and vibrant energies of the sun, sunstone stimulates personal power, creativity, strength, and leadership qualities. Associated with the sun god Ra, sunstone also brings the power of life, potential and possibilities, reflecting the confidence of the rich and famous. Connecting on this wavelength, wearers exude high energy, increase their social profile and attract opportunities for leadership, promotion or other good fortune.

Use sunstone in spellwork to step into the spotlight or shed light on an idea. This is useful when marketing a new business, pitching a concept or applying for a new job. Sunstone provides a burst of emotional strength in times of need. It may also help overcome loss, fearfulness or rejection.

Tiger's eye – courage
Negotiators, mediators and teachers benefit from the solar energies of courage, strength and willpower of tiger's eye. It helps you find the positive in any situation, increases feelings of optimism and builds resilience. For any magical working that requires sheer spirit of determination and perseverance, tiger's eye delivers solid vibrations of commitment to ensure the deed gets done.

Also known for its grounding energy, tiger's eye can assist with the healing of broken bones, durability against infection and prevention against being hurt. Wearing tiger's eye can build resilience and endurance in both the body and the mind so you remain calm, centred and focused.

Turquoise – the bridge
Connecting the elements of Air, Earth, Water and Spirit, turquoise is often worn for power, luck and protection. Especially when travelling, turquoise helps to protect against theft, prevents accidents, falls and even guards animals (such as horses) from going astray. Turquoise is said to provide the grounding needed to balance altruistic ideals, help identify unwise investments and assist in decision making. Carrying turquoise can help with reaching for the stars while keeping the feet firmly on the ground.

Genuine turquoise is so rare that care needs to be taken to avoid buying a fake. Spotting one isn't easy. Real turquoise is brittle, with varying shades of blue / green with grey, brown or black spiderweb-like lines of bedrock running through it. Often, howlite and magnesite (which are white, porous stones with matrix lines) are dyed, and sold at a fraction of the cost of genuine turquoise.

The majority of turquoise jewellery is coated in epoxy to make it stable during the cutting and polishing process, which unfortunately makes it feel very similar to plastic or resin imitations. To test, touch a piece of the stone to your lips, and scratch it gently with your teeth. Resin or plastic beads will be warm to touch, in contrast to mineral-based stones which will feel cooler. Howlite and magnesite are softer than turquoise and will scratch more easily, sometimes revealing the white under the dye, whereas turquoise has colour through the stone. However, if you simply cannot tell if the stone is fake or genuine, and cannot bring yourself to chip a corner off, you will have to rely on the supplier's honesty.

Creating crystal grids

Every natural pattern of growth or movement forms geometric shapes that can be calculated in mathematical code. The molecular patterns of crystals can be seen repeated in snowflakes, plant cells, animal DNA and the spiralling galaxies of the cosmos. The use of sacred geometry is an ancient practice that explores and explains the way the energy of creation organises itself, attracting and attaching to like patterns.

A crystal grid is a powerful tool which draws upon sacred geometry to combine and focus the energies of multiple crystals at the same time. Rather than wearing or carrying crystals for gentle radiating energy, placing specific crystals in particular patterns augments, transforms and directs stronger, focused energy towards goals, desires and intentions.

If you have a very clear intention (*why*) such as abundance, love, or achieving high results in an exam or work project, this will guide you to the crystal properties with corresponding energies (*what*). The shape of the grid will supercharge the direction of the energy (*how*).

Simple grid shapes can be set up with as few as four crystals; either multiple crystals of the same type, or a combination of different correspondences, depending on your goal. Ideally, when creating a crystal grid, a larger crystal is set in the centre with smaller ones placed in the outer part of the grid. The geometrical shape of the grid augments the properties of the individual crystals, in an ordered and systematic way from the focal crystal, to the supporting crystals and back to the central point. The energy flows and circles within the grid in perpetual motion (I like to include selenite to maintain a high level of charge in all the stones if I am leaving a grid for a long period of time). The more complex the geometrical pattern, the more varied the shapes, types and sizes of crystals, the more layers of energy you can add – but this takes practice and a good understanding of crystal properties and correspondences. Often, simple is better.

Once your crystals have been charged, select a grid shape for your requirements. Here are some options:

Triangles are simple structures that combine three main energy sources and focus upwards to a higher consciousness. Triangles and pyramids are the best shapes to sit or lie within to improve wellness, find balance and increase psychic or higher self-awareness.

Squares create boundaries to contain energy or keep energies out. They create a sense of grounding or a base to build upon. Squares often have other geometrical shapes layered over them. Bedrooms and property boundaries benefit from simple squares to keep love in and trespassers out.

Circles are possibly the oldest, strongest and most used shape. By creating boundaries of protection and focus of energy in the same way as overlaying a triangle with a square, circles create a sense of safety, security and unity. Mandalas and circular flower layouts are examples of more complex overlapping circles, which draw on multiple, external points, refracting and reflecting the energies and redirecting inwards. The more intricate the overlaying of circles, the more intense and focussed the energy. Mandalas are inspirational and therapeutic, merging inner and outer worlds to allow you to explore your inner self and express feelings.

Spirals work differently to circles because they radiate energy in ever expanding, outward waves, whilst also drawing energy back into the focal point. This shape is useful to manifest intentions by offering them to the universal energy of the cosmos and attracting energies of the same frequency back to the source.

Stars are made from overlapping triangles to create high spiritual and psychic energy for healing, protection or connecting with spirit guides.

After you have mindfully placed your crystals into your chosen grid shape, you need to activate it. To activate the grid, your intention should be spoken clearly into the space, although it can alternatively be written on paper or carved on a central candle. If spoken, chanted or intoned out loud, the vibrations are picked up by the crystals, amplified and carried with purpose. State your intentions in a way that is meaningful to you. For example, with a triangle of blue lace agate surrounded by a circle of citrine, place one hand on your throat and the other on your solar plexus and state:

"I have created this grid to connect me with my courage to deliver the speech next Friday with confidence and intelligence."

Leave your grid in place for a predetermined time. Each time you pass by the grid, remind yourself of its purpose and recharge it with your energy while stating your intention. Leaving a crystal grid by the window or living plants will add solar, lunar and living energies when you aren't close by.

As with all natural/found objects like rocks, shells, seedpods or flowers, the benefits of merging energies are formed from close interactions. The secret language of crystals (energy) is revealed when we tune into their vibrations and when they raise ours.

I've Been Hexed or Cursed. Please Help!

Some friends of mine own an esoteric shop. They told me that the most frequent concerns from shop visitors were: *"I think I've been cursed (or hexed). How do I know and how can I stop it?"*

Here are some of the reasons why people think they have been cursed or hexed:
- lots of bad luck
- negative and obsessive thinking
- extreme emotions and mood swings
- nightmares
- body aches or pain, or headaches
- feeling depleted, drained and exhausted for no apparent reason
- the feeling of being watched or observed
- a pressure on shoulders / chest
- losing things
- being accident prone
- 'weird' illnesses
- feeling lousy after someone tells you they've cursed or hexed you.

A curse or hex results from deliberate action. That's how it differs from a psychic attack, because with the right circumstances, anyone with a powerful charge of emotions can unintentionally release a psychic attack. Being the victim of a curse or hex implies that someone with magical knowledge is specifically and maliciously out to harm you.

The bottom line is that curses or hexes are extremely rare and rarely effective unless performed by a practitioner who knows their business. In Australia, there probably aren't too many folk who could be bothered doing a routine curse working in response to a minor insult or transgression.

Simple curse or psychic attack busters

Here are some relatively simple ideas about what to do if you feel you have been cursed or are the victim of psychic attack:

+ Laugh a lot and enjoy yourself. As George Herbert wrote in 1610, *'living well is the best revenge.'*
+ Add salt to your bath water or scrub yourself with salt while showering. Cleanse your auric system.
+ Spend time in sunlight (using sun-safe practices of course). If possible, lie on your back, on the earth, in the sun. Soak up those energies.
+ Seal off and magically protect your bedroom, then the external entrances to your home and finally the entire perimeter. See the *Energetic Cleansing* chapter for more information.
+ If things are really bad and there is a personal link to the house (such as a toxic flat-mate), move out for a while – or move that person out.
+ Wear or hang Mediterranean 'eye' symbols in prominent locations.
+ Wear a suitable, protective crystal such as tiger's eye.
+ Visualise harmful energies returning to their sender.
+ Imagine your aura as a super-strong interlocked steel shell or reflective mirror surrounding you – impenetrable.
+ Call on your spirit guide for protection.
+ Block or unfriend on social media if that is the source of the connection. Stop it cold. Have a social media detox.

Mirror magic

Mirrors have a useful role in protective magic, when you feel you are the target of negative energies, or there seems to be a lot of unfortunate events occurring in your life. Because mirrors are reflective, with willed intention, mirrors can magically disperse or direct energies back to the sender. Try wearing mirrored jewellery, or place a special mirror onto your altar.

Putting a mirror on the outside of your house can help reflect energies back to their source and bedazzle passers-by. If you are the recipient of unwanted, strong emotions from others, a quick 'self-defence' tip is to visualise yourself encased in a massive, egg-shaped reflective mirror.

Parting thoughts

In some cases, the appropriate response is to keep a diary of times, dates and conversations rather than trying to engage in a *Lord of the Rings*-style magical battle with another person. Gather photographic evidence. And talk to the police, as some matters require a physical or legal response. You may also like to seek professional assistance to support any emergent mental health issues. Wonderful resources are available online, but sometimes the best solution is to arrange a face-to-face consultation with a qualified practitioner, such as a clinical psychologist.

Energetic Cleansing

By Jacq Hackett

Universal energy
Witches see the interconnectedness of everything around us and work with the energy of nature. As a witch, working with the alignment and harmony of the rhythms of the universe, you may be called to work with the community in healing ceremonies. Witches use energetic cleansings to welcome or bless new members of the community; cure a person or land of illness; and create a sacred space to contact spirits, ancestors and deities.

Rationalists without a deep connection to spirit and universal energy argue that such rituals no longer hold a place in the modern world. Modern sciences (with perhaps the exception of psychology which, like witchcraft, is unable to provide scientific measurements of provable truth) describe the practice of energetic cleansing as new age or a hippie fad. Those who investigate spiritual energy from a purely clinical perspective, separate themselves from the complete spectrum of their abilities, potential and power. A connection with flowing universal energy is forged at an intimate level, not merely academic.

Reconnecting to the flow and rhythm of the divine allows you to reach your full potential, reclaim your power and do so without unnecessary strain. When you are connected, you are supported by powerful energies at the right time, you gain insight, and can restore your vitality. When universal energy is flowing freely, you can accomplish things that need to be accomplished in an easy and effortless way.

Sensing energy
Have you ever walked into a room and felt the tension? Perhaps you instantly knew an argument had recently occurred or that the people in the room were unhappy. This is an example of energy sensing.

If that same room was the scene of many arguments or ongoing complaints over an extended period of time, the stale and stagnant energy will linger, multiply and bring everybody's mood down. It becomes a sickness and can manifest mentally and physically.

Your body is a primary indicator of the quality of the energy around you. Common ways of sensing these energy shifts is by intuition, a gut feeling, tingling sensations, or the rising of hair. It is not an intellectual process. It is a felt sense. By acknowledging your everyday encounters with the energy around you, you will increase your receptivity and sensitivity to subtle environmental cues

When energy feels stuck or off-centre, energetic cleansing heals simultaneously at the physical, emotional and spiritual levels. It is a ritualized action to encourage energy to flow freely, like running water – without blockages. Connecting to and realigning energy is deeply healing for both practitioner and participant. Redirecting energy can therefore be seen as the healing of negative energy in a place, such as a home, an office, a piece of land; or the negative energy surrounding a person. This flows from their thoughts and emotions, or can manifest as physical symptoms of illness.

Working with energy

It is interesting that Pagan traditions tend to use natural, found, raw materials in nature or outdoor temples; whereas Abrahamic religions have adopted more refined and gilded tools to use within the house of God. Whether using burning embers or censers, flowing streams or fonts, sacred land or cathedrals, the intent is to use elemental tools in a spiritual ritual to connect with the divine energy of the Universe to create change – such as finding peace, joy, abundance. The elemental energy patterns within the cosmos can be seen on a molecular level repeated throughout nature in snowflakes, plant cells and animal and human DNA. These vibrations attract others on the same frequency, connecting different hosts. As a witch you will have experienced a sense of peace and tranquillity when in nature. The connection you feel is the realignment of your own energy source with the divine.

Space cleansing ritual

The first step in a cleansing ritual is the mindful collection of supplies and tools. You are going to be a conduit of energy, so preparation of your body as the main tool in the ritual takes precedence. Take your time. Do your best to slow down and not rush through this first step. As with any pre-ritual preparations, a period of fasting, bathing and meditation aids the physical, mental, emotional and spiritual grounding that is required to become present and disconnected from your everyday thoughts and emotions.

See what works best to put you into the right frame of mind: I enjoy an early morning surf, a walk amongst trees or spending time in my vegetable garden. Take a shower right before the space clearing session and be sure to put on fresh clean clothes. Meditate for at least five minutes to calm your mind and heart – longer if possible. If another person will be present during the ritual, encourage them to join you, both in grounding and cleansing the area during the ceremony.

Mindfully gather the sacred tools and materials for the ritual. Herb bundles, depending on the main ingredient, are designed to smoulder and burn slowly. Whilst we do not want a flaming torch, herb bundles at least need to smoke. Mugwort is especially good in keeping embers lit and smoking if your bundle doesn't burn well.

Light a candle and keep it nearby. The candle flame can be used to light and relight the same end of the herb bundle during the cleansing ceremony. Hold it down for flames to ignite and take hold, then upright to smoke and smoulder.

A small bowl or plate should be held underneath the herb bundle to catch any ashes or embers. In smaller areas where there is a risk of setting off fire alarms, it may be prudent to use a charcoal disc with incense shavings and dried herbs in a censor or mini cauldron. You can use sand or black salt to properly extinguish the embers safely after the ritual is complete.

Allow enough space and time for the ritual so you don't feel rushed. If you have another person assisting you, prepare some simple cleansing tools such as bells, feathers or salted water they can use while you are smoke cleansing. Before you start, confirm with others in the ritual what the cleansing ceremony is to achieve.

If your wish is for your home and family to be a safe, loving space, you will want to create a newly cleared space and then welcome your intentions into the energetic void created. This is especially beneficial if the home was recently purchased from another family. You will want to sweep the space clear of residual energies that contributed to the family moving out and imprint your own. Sometimes the intention is to provide healing, clarity or peace of mind and a single room may be cleansed – such as a bedroom or study. The denser energies of illness, fear or anxiety (from sleeplessness, nightmares or an upcoming exam) can be cleansed and replaced with the lighter energies of health, calm and understanding. Once the intention of what energy is to be transformed is made clear, it is time to begin.

Cast a circle or visualise a bubble of protective light around yourself and other ritual participants. Call upon the elements and the divine to aid, guide and protect you.

Protected and armed with mindfulness, tools and intention, begin at the main entrance, and move around the inside of the home with your smouldering herb bundle (or incense). Move mindfully, purposefully with steady intent, anti-clockwise to banish, or clockwise to create energy around the entire home. Keep those intentions clearly and firmly in your mind. Clear and fill. Neutralise and create. Negative out, positive in. Raise one hand to the corners of each room, from the floor to the ceiling and get a sense of the energy shift. If you sense stubborn energy, increase your own by clapping your hands together or forcefully directing your intent through sound.

Sounds and vibrations assist with shifting energy so a second person can ring a bell, sound a singing bowl or vocalise to restore harmony by simultaneously destroying, creating and maintaining energy in every part of the home.

Alternatively, there are spiritual and religious chants that can be used to augment intent. As with any enchantment, heed the wording – witches manifest intent by speaking/thinking things into existence – and be sure to understand the meaning behind any words you are not familiar with. Two of my personal favourites are:

"Gods above and Gods below
Cast all evil from this home.
Peace and protection, may they come.
As I do say, it shall be done."

I use this easy-to-remember chant when asking homeowners to join in and:

"Divine energy take from this space:
ego jealousy
want
ignorance
and attachment united in hatred.
Divine energy fill this space with:
generosity
ethics
patience
understanding
and freedom united in love."

A friend of mine, Tenzin (a monk and security detail for the current Dalai Lama) translated the Buddhist mantra *Om mani padme hum* (the Jewel is in the Lotus) into English for me. I have found that if I repeat sounds or words for which I have no understanding, there is less of a connection to their energy. I felt this acutely when repeating "namaste" in Nepal. Even though I knew the translation means '*I see you*', it wasn't until a local explained it meant "*my soul sees and recognises your soul and we are the same*", that the full power of those words were felt.

When chanting a spell, it is always best to create one specifically for the cleansing intent. This is especially important when performing a cleansing for another person. Invite the homeowner to join in to impress their energy upon the property. The simpler the ritual, the better. Do not become distracted by words when it is the intent and energetic healing that is important.

Keep at least one window open for stale energy to leave and fresh energy to enter. Make sure that smoke drifts down around doorways and windows, into hard-to-reach areas, dark corners and hidden nooks. If there are stairs, go up or down when you reach them, always moving in the same direction, to return to the main entrance. It is optional to continue the cleansing ritual beyond the internal boundaries to the external borders of the property. Ever increasing circles around the home create stronger energy alignment.

When you arrive back at the entrance, speak your intention one last time to close the ritual and douse the herb bundle, visualising the entire property glowing with bright blue-white light. Any residual energy will be attached to yourself and the tools used. It is important to remove yourself from the property and shake it off. Stomping your feet and slapping your clothes down while visualising any negativity dissolving into the air or ground will do until you can properly cleanse and re-energise.

Keep your tools sacred by using them only for rituals and not mundane activities. It is useful to view your tools as weapons against negative forces. You may feel drawn to display them on your altar. Alternatively, store your tools and materials in a spell chest away from negative energy and cleanse or re-energise them before and after use.

There are no time restrictions on cleansing and rituals can be performed regularly. It is a beautiful technique to use on yourself, refresh a space or repurpose a room. However, a deep, full house clearing is recommended at least once a year or after an intense negative event, such as a divorce. An energetic cleanse can be done when you first move into a home, seasonally (such as a Spring clean) or before an auspicious event, such as studying for an exam or preparing for a baby.

After the cleanse

Like wilting flowers when life energy is spent, your own body may be battered after the cleansing ritual. There is a 'coming down' period after being bombarded with a lot of psychic and energetic information during the process. It is important to ground and recover as quickly as possible. Eating helps. Sit in a quiet cafe. If the property is your own, it is better to prepare a snack prior to the ritual and eat it beyond the boundary. As you 'come down', take time to honour and process any pertinent information you picked up on during the cleansing in this separate, neutral space.

When you recover and return to the freshly cleansed space, you will feel the energetic shift and be able to pick up on the subtleties of energy. The aim is to have clarity and a sense of peace as you move through the newly cleansed home. Take note of any gut feelings where the energy may still be off. It is totally alright to relight the herb bundle and revisit a room if you are feeling up to it.

Whilst there are no limits on re-cleansing the home, there will be limits on what you can handle. Feel free to explore your strength and style after thoroughly recovering. Once you are conscious of these, the cleansing process becomes your own, in line with your own energy. You will know when and how often to cleanse. You will feel and connect to the flow of energies around you. You will connect with the method and tools that resonate highest with you. The rest will flow effortlessly. After all, we aren't working against energy, we are working with it.

Suggestions for smoke cleansing

The smoke from plants, resins, bark and minerals has healing and restorative qualities and can be used ceremoniously to prepare the witch for ritual. The curling swirls of smoke part the veil between the worlds, form a bridge to another plane, and carry intention out to the universe. While the inhalation of smoke may not in itself be mind-altering, whether fragrant or pungent, the scent acts as a trigger to inspire memories, induce emotions and awaken a sense of direction or knowing. When combined with chanting, singing and dancing, the witch effectively enters an altered state of consciousness. The sacred practice of smoke cleansing is a vivid spiritual experience for both practitioner and participants.

Energetic cleansing in witchcraft is practiced from a deep understanding of the way energy works. Because all things vibrate on some molecular level creating energy, the power within all things can be retained, released and transformed. In burning plant substances, the powerful energy of fire unleashes the healing energy of the plant to neutralize and purify negative presence.

Plants associated with purity and healing are often used in ritual cleansing. Even after being harvested, plants retain a life source that resonates throughout its cells – fresh or dried. As witches, we mindfully access their energy by absorbing nutrients enhanced by the quality of sunshine, rain, air and soil (the elements), whether internally as a food source or inhalant, or topically as a salve. So, it is imperative to harvest only what is needed, without damaging the ecosystem and with the spiritual intention of using it as a ritual offering or gateway. It is impossible to guarantee this when purchased online or from the local yoga studio. So, buy mindfully from reputable, local sources (such as *The Witches Apothecary*) if you're not able to wildcraft or harvest your own homegrown sacred plants and herbs.

Whilst sage is commonly used, it is not particularly aromatic. It is generally used before and after healing sessions to remove negative energy that may linger in spaces, people and any tools used in ritual. Popular alternatives to sage are lavender, mugwort, sandalwood, rosemary and even orange peel. These more fragrant plants can be woven into purchased herb bundles, or bound fresh and dried if you are making your own. Knowledge of the energetic properties, correspondences and medicinal values of the plants you intend to use gives a greater focus to the intent of the cleansing.

Lavender is often used for its gentle energies associated with relaxation. The ancient Romans used the heady scent in bath water, perfumes and teas to assist in both relaxation and healing. An energetic realignment using dried lavender is powerful in bedrooms, the bathroom and any area that feels too tightly wound up (which includes ourselves).

Manna or Australian sweetgrass, native to the moist and cooler climates of southern Australia, has a gentle energy about it. Excellent as a tea with a soft vanilla scent, sweetgrass helps the mind clear, the body relax and generate a sense of peace. If you have already cleansed an area, following up with dried sweetgrass is useful to welcome fresh energy. Use in small but higher traffic areas such as a kitchenette or apartment living room.

Mugwort's scent is stronger and so too is its energy. Associated with Artemis the moon goddess, mugwort is a powerful energy realignment for women. Known to regulate moon flow or menstrual cycles, the smoke from mugwort is especially potent for relaxing the pelvis muscles and other tired muscles.

Please do not use if there are pregnant women in the home. Otherwise, it can be used in every room in the house.

Sandalwood has been revered for thousands of years for its aroma and medicinal properties. The captivating scent of the heartwood outlasts many other plants and its oil has been prized above all others. Associated with beauty and sex, sandalwood is often used to energetically realign the bedroom. However, the tree is parasitic in nature and should be used in moderation or as a base for another plant.

Rosemary is well known for its association with memories and ancestors. Used for over 8000 years (in written history), the energy released from rosemary is associated with remembrance and can aid in past life regression or ancestral work. Dried rosemary bundles burn well and fragrantly for use inside or outside. It is best used in harmony with house/land spirits, not for banishings.

Dried orange peel has all the zesty energy of the ripe fruit. In complete opposition to rosemary, orange peel is associated with new life and fresh energy. As such, an energetic cleansing with orange peel is perfect for moving into new accommodations, refreshing second-hand furniture, or for laser-focus and concentration in the study or office.

There are many other dried plants that can be used in herb bundles. Combinations of herbs, leaves and flowers give depth to cleansing rituals and blend fragrances to suit the energies required. Look to your own garden for inspiration. Living in Australia we have easy access to **eucalyptus** – one of the most healing plants on the planet. Cinnamon sticks, incense or resins such as frankincense or myrrh are another way to work with the healing and purifying energies of fire and plant medicines.

Alternatives to smoke cleansing

While smoke cleansing is one of the easiest ways to improve the energy of a space, it's not always the best method. Some people are highly sensitive to smoke or have allergies to fragrant, flowering herbs. Some herbs when dried burn all too well and are a fire hazard. Plus, modern smoke alarms simply kill the mood if they go off mid cleansing. Thankfully, there's more than one way to connect with universal energy and cleanse an area. If smoke cleansing does not appeal to you, consider these popular alternatives.

Smoke-free methods include salt water, essential oil diffusers or mist sprays. You can also use the convenience of fresh organic matter like oranges. The act of peeling the skin from an orange releases the energy and fragrance into the air. When making your own potions, stay mindful of your intent when adding salt to water, essential oil into alcohol or while peeling or misting.

The physical plane includes restrictions such as walls, furniture and other physical boundaries. Universal energy permeates everything from the energy inside our bodies, as well as the energy inside and outside structures. Similarly, the vibrational energy of sound radiates through solid objects, dense spaces and bodies.

Using a singing bowl (or similar tool), not only shifts the energy in your home, but also your own personal energy. Needing two hands and a clear mind, gently strike the bowl and, slowly but firmly, run the side of the mallet in a circular motion against the rim. Deep sounding bowls/bells are great for around the home. Hanging windchimes outside the house uses the same principle as you can use the vibrations to transform negative energies from the other side of a wall or building. Similarly, music, singing, chants or affirmations can shift the energy. If you don't have bells and prefer not to sing, hum. Simple sounds lift one's spirit and connect to the universal source of all vibration.

Another earthly form of energy vibration comes from crystals and semi-precious gemstones. Commonly used crystals in the home are rose quartz (due to associations with love, peace and harmony) and clear quartz (due to versatility and healing, cleansing powers). Black tourmaline in your home is also useful as a protective stone to absorb and balance energies. Placing crystals beside a bed, around a room or the entire property can act as an energetic matrix. Mist can be made from placing a crystal into a spray bottle with water and used instead of smoke. However, care must be taken as some crystals are water-soluble. For more information see the chapter on crystals.

High energy items such as fresh flowers, plants and indoor gardens bring vibrant energies to homes and can be brought into any room of the house. Energy likes to move freely, so the act of clearing, cleaning, decluttering and general tidying opens the space for natural flow. As with all tools, remember to swap out wilting flowers, re-energise crystals, play uplifting music, top up oil diffusers and renew your own intentions to keep the energy in your home flowing.

Divination

By Sandra Greenhalgh

Divination helps us foretell potential future outcomes and gain insight into current or past events. We then have the option of using those intuitions for guidance to make the best decisions possible.

Divination was practiced in most ancient civilizations and is still as relevant today for the modern witch. That's likely because it is part of the human condition to wonder about the future, or what comes next. It's also a survival skill – the ability to read social and environmental signposts regarding war, leadership, plague or famine was once the difference between life and death. As well as these practical matters, honing your divination skills helps to strengthen your intuition and connection with the otherworlds.

The word *divination* has the same source as the word *divine*. This infers that a greater intelligence or wisdom is involved in the process of divination, rather than just (potentially flawed) human logic. Divination is not a rational process. A genuine divinatory reading doesn't involve the reader pondering things through in a logical manner. It can be surprising (or shocking at times), illuminating and quite uncanny.

Are divinatory readings 100% accurate? Not at all. And this is where we enter 'free will vs predestination' territory. Most diviners will explain that we are not absolutely trapped by a predetermined fate (destiny). We do have the ability to shape our lives to some extent (free will). Due to that precarious balance of destiny and free will, not all predictions will occur, which is actually a bit of a relief, really. But a great reading provides us with the opportunity to change how we interact with current situations, which in turn impacts our future options.

Not everyone wants to use the opportunities for change they learn about in a divination session. Sometimes people don't – or can't – heed sensible advice if it contradicts their current perceptions or if taking action feels too difficult. It's certainly frustrating for diviners when someone keeps looking for different answers to the same question over a short period of time. Often the answer will remain the same, no matter how many readings you have.

At times, querents (person seeking a reading) attend a divination session because they want to feel reassured, or to talk about themselves in a safe situation. And, in my opinion, this service can be just as relevant for the querent.

Tips to improve your readings

- I'm sure you won't be surprised by the first recommendation, which is practise, practise, practise! Experience is literally the best teacher. It's only through practise that you can hone your skills. Both good and bad readings help you become a better reader.
- Look after your tools. I often ask people to wash their hands before touching my Tarot cards. I also perform a simple 'cleansing' between readings and before I pack them away. My favourite technique is to flick across the ends of the cards while imaging any stray energies flying off into the aether.
- Pay attention to how the question or query is framed. A poorly articulated query will facilitate an inaccurate or messy reading. It's also best to avoid questions that require a 'yes' or 'no' response if your divination tool isn't designed to provide such answers. The pendulum is fairly useful in this case, the Tarot less so.
- If you are reading for someone else, deliberately 'unlink' from your querent after completion. Stand up, shake your body, have a drink.
- Keep records. Compare and measure your readings with 'real world' occurrences and take note of the feedback from your querents. This will enable you to discern valid insights in comparison to 'fake news'.
- Don't take things too literally or get stuck on the technicalities. Divination is not a precise science.
- Be careful about setting accurate timeframes. Providing accurate time forecasts with most divination tools can be difficult, although astrology can be an exception. I had a reading once where the reader told me quite specific timelines – and the predicted events happened three years later than foretold. Oops.
- Create an environment which is peaceful and conducive to divination, particularly when you are learning. With practice, you can perform a reading in any setting, even when your market stall flies away in a thunderstorm. (Yes, I speak from personal experience).

✦ Whatever tool you choose to use, learn it thoroughly. Research it. Live with it. Then when you know it completely, focus more on the inner, Spirit connection that enables an eerily accurate reading. This sometimes will completely negate the visible message of the tool.

Divination tools

Divination practices and tools vary enormously. From throwing animal bones onto the ground, considering the flight patterns of birds, to clicking on a phone app to electronically draw the card of the day, the range of divination tools seems almost endless. Some people prefer not to use a physical implement when performing divinatory readings, and that's their call. However, there are many benefits to using divination tools, such as Tarot or oracle cards.

Tools help to focus the reader. An appropriate tool helps you to access the relevant imagery and symbolism and bring back divinatory messages to share. They also help you close down psychic connections; put away your tool and it's a clear message you are no longer 'open for business'. I'm a big fan of using a divination tool for this precise reason. A tool also acts as in interface, enabling us to journey behind the veil separating the mundane world from the otherworlds. Generally, the more you use a tool, the more adept you become with it, and the better you can understand your tool, the better you can perceive the information relayed to you.

Here's some divination tools and methods (in alphabetical order) to get you started:

Astrology
While it takes a long time to learn, astrology can be used as a powerful divinatory tool for predicting the future. In particular, horary astrology answers specific questions with great precision. One of the strengths of divining with astrology is that timing is implicit to the art.

Automatic writing
Automatic writing is the process of changing consciousness and allowing your hand to write or draw as it pleases. I'm not too fond of this form of divination. It might be quite effective as a conduit for messages from the 'spirit plane', or it can be wishy-washy and difficult to disengage from afterwards. Think about it: what or who are you connecting with when seeking advice using the medium of automatic writing?

Bibliomancy

Bibliomancy is the practice of randomly choosing a page, line or passage in a book to provide you with guidance. It's quick and can be surprisingly accurate!

Dowsing

Through dowsing, it is possible to locate water, minerals or geomantic energy fields which are located under (or through) the surface of the earth. Most dowsers use two dowsing rods or a forked stick. It's easy to create your own homemade dowsing rods by cutting then bending two wire coat hangers into 'L' shapes and making handles by cutting pieces of plastic hose.

Hold one rod in each hand by the handle, with the wire pointing forward, at waist level and shoulder width apart. Walk slowly across the section of earth you are exploring. Those with 'the knack' will see the rods moving from a straight position to crossing over. Dowsing seems to work really effectively for some people, while others get no response at all from the dowsing rods.

Dreams

Learning to interpret dreams is a valuable facet of divination. Recurring dreams that repeat over more than one night are particularly significant. Perhaps you are being sent a message and didn't listen properly the first time around, so the Universe wants you to take notice. Dictionaries to interpret the symbolism of dreams are available freely online. However, it's crucial to reflect on the personal meaning of the symbolism to you. How does it make you feel? What are your personal associations with the images experienced while dreaming?

Oracle cards

I love oracle cards almost as much as I love Tarot cards! I even created a deck, called the *Druid Wisdom Oracle*, because I value the flexibility and insights that oracle cards offer.

Unlike Tarot decks, there can be any number of cards included in an oracle deck. The best thing about oracle cards is that you can often pick up a deck and use them straight away without the need to first learn a complex system. My preferred methods of working with oracle cards are:

- ✦ Pick a single card to gain insights or spark your intuition.
- ✦ Choose three cards. One to signify past influences, one for present circumstances and one for potential future outcomes.

✦ Finish a Tarot reading by asking the querant to choose one oracle card. Tarot readings can be gritty and deeply engaging interactions. Ending with a single oracle card can help 'set an intention' and round off the divination session.

Ouija boards
Generally, I advise against the serious, committed use of a Ouija board unless you have confidence in the people around you, and know how to effectively banish or close down afterwards. Most of the time, stories of haunted Ouija board sessions are the urban legends of teenagers. They are not intrinsically scary or haunted, nor are they particularly effective as divination tools.

Pendulum
A pendulum is a simple and effective divination tool and can be used to locate people, artefacts, substances or provide accurate yes/no responses. It's easy enough to create one in a few minutes by attaching an item (the 'bob') to the end of a semi-flexible length of rope or chain. For example, you can use a necklace with a pendant, or pick up a short stick and tie it onto the end of a piece of string. Some people keep designated and consecrated pendulums such as a shaped crystal on a chain, but it is not necessary to buy an expensive item to receive an accurate response.

To begin your pendulum session, ascertain what kind of swing or movement means *no* and *yes*. Do this by holding the far end of the cord or chain between forefinger and thumb and ask aloud: *"What is the sign for yes?"* Relax and watch the pendulum for movement. It may rock back and forth or swing around in a circle. When you have received a response you are satisfied with, still the movements with your other hand. Then ask: *"What is the sign for no?"* Once again, relax and watch how the pendulum moves. Do this every time before you use a pendulum.

Psychometry
Psychometry is the ability to interpret energies connected with an object or artefact, including rooms or buildings. For psychometry to be effective, you need to be in close physical proximity with the object, ideally holding it with your hand. After a period of centering and stillness, open your awareness to psychically receive messages. The information might be transmitted via images, words or emotions. As with all divination techniques, validating the information you receive is vital, so it's a good idea to perform some test-runs first to hone your skills.

Runes
Runes are sets of letters from Germanic languages, frequently associated with the Vikings. The rune shapes can be used in magical workings as well as a direct and unambiguous divination system.

Scrying
Gazing into a reflective surface helps you to enter an altered state of consciousness and potentially see pertinent images. You can scry with any reflective surface, such as a black mirror, still water or a shiny crystal. Staring into fire or a candle flame is another effective scrying technique, as it defocuses your eyes and relaxes your mind. You don't need expensive props such as a pure crystal sphere and it's easy to make your own black mirror by painting the back of the glass surface.

To be honest, I'm a scrying dud. It just doesn't work for me. Try as much as I can, I just can't see any little pictures like some people claim to see.

Tarot
The Tarot is a popular divination tool among witches. Decks have 78 cards which contain a myriad of symbolic and historical meanings. Tarot is my go-to divination tool. Unfortunately, it is beyond the scope of this book to provide detailed information on the many ways in which Tarot can be used. There are literally hundreds of books and resources available. My favourite book is *Super Tarot* by Sasha Fenton, and I recommend the *Global Spiritual Studies* website for online resources.

Tea leaf reading
What a wonderful divinatory art! There's something so homely about having a cuppa, then having your tea leaves read. Each pattern of tea leaves can tell a story, and there are many online resources available to help decipher the meaning of the images seen inside the cup.

FESTIVALS: Rituals and Ceremonies

This section provides suggestions on how to create a ritual, based on The Circle Coven's methods. These have been adapted for a small group or solitary witch. Feel welcome to modify the suggestions to suit your personalised needs.

Detailed, coven-specific information about rituals and ceremonies is included in The Circle Coven *section.*

Crafting a Solitary or Small Group Ritual

'Symbols and ritual acts are used to trigger altered states of consciousness, in which insights that go beyond words are revealed.'
Starhawk in *The Spiral Dance: A Rebirth of the Ancient Religion of the Great Goddess.*

Steps to a solitary or small group ritual

When witches talk about doing a ritual, we are referring to a ceremony (or *rite*) involving magick and the mystical, undertaken at a specific time, with deliberate actions leading to desired outcomes.

Any of the following steps can be adjusted or omitted as you please, in accordance with your preferences. For a detailed description about how The Circle Coven does things, see the *Circle Coven Ritual* chapter.

Here are simple points to get you started with creating your own rituals:
1. Choose a location where you won't be interrupted. Physically prepare the space, for example, pick up sticks or sharp stones if you are outside or declutter the floor if inside.
2. Set up your altar if you wish to use one, in your preferred location. There are more details about altar set up in the next section.
3. Create your sacred space by casting the circle.
4. Invite or acknowledge the quarters or directional aspects. This could include (for example) East, South, West, North; Air, Fire, Water, Earth, and Spirit; or earth, sea and sky.
5. Invite or acknowledge the Gods, spirit allies, or ancestors.
6. Perform your magical working or meditation.
7. Bless food and fluid, and then eat and drink.
8. Farewell the Gods, spirit allies, or ancestors.
9. Farewell the quarters or directional aspects.
10. Release the boundary of your circle by stepping through it and seeing it 'pop' or visualise it dissolving into the Universe.
11. Tidy up and put away your equipment.

12. Ground yourself.
13. Write in your magical diary.

Casting the circle
The circle is the church of the Craft. Weather and other factors permitting, the circle is created on the earth itself as our witchcraft is a nature-centred practice. The size of the circle can be anything from one metre in diameter and upwards. While nine foot (2.75m) in diameter is traditional, the size of your circle depends on the number of participants and the space available rather than an exact measurement.

The boundary of the circle may be outlined with a cord or chalk or white sand, or any inert natural substance which will not harm the surface on which you are working. The coven's absolute favourite substance is white flour, as it is organic and highly visible at night. Salt will kill the grass, so we don't use it straight, with the exception of a tiny pinch diluted in water. Sometimes we mark the boundary of the circle with tea lights. With practice, this physical marking of the boundary of the circle is not necessary, but it's handy until you become used to the size of your space.

To create a circle in a new or unfamiliar location, place a stick or rock (or person) in the centre. Attach one end of your cord (or a piece of rope) to the central point, and while keeping a consistent distance from it, walk around holding the other end of the rope and mark out the boundary of your circle. After that, stand in the centre and locate the North, South, East and West points, using a compass. These days it's easy, as smart phones have a compass built in, so you don't need to travel with a separate compass in your ritual bag.

You don't need a fancy sword or athame to mark the boundary of your magical circle. A nicely formed stick picked up from the ground can be equally as effective – or best of all, use your body. Extend the index finger (or index and second finger) of your dominant hand. Hold your hand out from your body, walk around inside your boundary and visualise energy flowing out of the end of your athame/fingers/stick to seal the edge of your newly created magical space.

The Altar

For the solitary witch, your personal altar can be as simple or elaborate as you please. It may be located in any quarter or direction meaningful to you or convenient for the available space. You can create multiple altars if you like. As usual, I advocate for safety, so don't leave incense or candles burning unless it's safe to do so; and be mindful that crystals left in sunlight can act as a lens to start a fire. The items you place on your altar are also completely up to you. Experiment to discover what works best.

An altar can be as uncomplicated as a piece of cloth placed upon the ground, or a candle and a statue grouped together. For coven rituals, we usually use a small, light table with folding legs, which we cover with a cloth. This kind of altar is easily transportable and at a convenient height to minimise the need to bend down to equipment. During rituals, our coven altar table is placed in the North.

Within the coven, we have proscribed locations for the standard ritual items on the altar. This is quite helpful on dark nights (so you don't fumble around trying to find things!) and it also provides a sense of continuity. Here is a list of the items we consistently put upon our altar for coven rituals, and where we place them:

- ✦ *An altar cloth.* This can be a standard cloth for every ritual, or different ones in appropriate colours and designs for the ritual or season. Our current altar cloth is made of black felt with The Circle Coven emblem on the front, and from time to time we have to get it professionally dry cleaned to remove the build-up of melted wax. It can get pretty messy.
- ✦ *Goddess and God candles.* Candles are inscribed with the triple moon symbol for Goddess and a circle topped with horns for the God. We prefer to use large white pillar candles which are relit for each ritual. The candles are dressed prior to use (refer to the *Candle Magick* section). The Goddess candle is on your left when you stand behind the altar (with your back to the circle boundary); the God candle is on your right.

- **Pentacle.** This can be made of any flattish earthen or metal material. The one the coven currently uses is made of lightweight metal, about 20 cm in diameter. The pentacle is placed at the centre-front of the altar.
- **Plate.** Upon the pentacle we usually put the plate which holds the food for 'cakes and ale'.
- **Incense or charcoal burner.** We use a censor to burn charcoal blocks and herbs or incense. Our ritual gear includes a set of consecrated tongs to help set charcoal blocks alight without burning fingers. For years, we used a round swinging censor, similar to the ones used in Catholic churches. It was a wicked trap for the novice witch, as the lid and chains required scrupulous manipulations to prevent sizzled hands and the lid from falling off. We now use a shallow brass bowl, which rests on a bed of insulating material such as clay-based kitty litter or river sand. It's not perfect either. Maybe one day we will find the perfect censor. We place the censor on the right side of the altar (the same side as the God candle).
- **Chalice.** The coven uses a large cup, filled with an appropriate beverage such as port or mead. We also store additional 'ale' in a vessel under the altar in case the chalice needs to be topped up! The coven's current clay chalice was created by a lovely witch who lives on the Gold Coast. After many years of use and haphazard storage, the stem recently snapped off at the base. However, we decided we like it better that way, so instead of reattaching the stem, the chalice-bowl now sits flat and securely on the left side of the altar (near the Goddess candle).
- **Wand.** We do not use a wand in rituals unless specifically required. This is probably due to habit more than anything, as we tend to use the coven sword for casting the circle. I'm sure there's a joke in there about not having a wand present during women-only rituals.
- **Three little bowls for oil, salt, and water.** These bowls are put in the middle of the altar. We add oil to the red bowl, water to the blue bowl and coarse sea salt to the green bowl. Occasionally we place these bowls at the quarter points rather than on the altar. The type of oil varies. Sometimes we use oil purposely and ritually created. Other times, we raid Scarlet's ritual cupboard for whatever is there. Sometimes members forget to take home their bottles of essential oil, and they somehow find their way into the ritual box.
- **A bell.** The bell is located on the right side of the altar. We don't always use a bell in ritual, but it can be useful to signal different stages of the

ritual, or as an attention getter if the witches get unruly. That's a joke, by the way. Our witches are rarely unruly during ritual – except when they need to be.

- **Representations of the divine or elemental correspondences.** These can be statues, carvings, or special natural objects such as shells or antlers. Use varies from ritual to ritual and the waxing and waning enthusiasms of coven members.

- **The sword.** The coven sword leans against the front of the altar, with the point down. We used to have a *massive* coven sword, courtesy of Scarlet who fought in medieval society clubs. However, the heavy, authentic sword was too unwieldy, so we've reverted to a smaller, lighter sword. It still looks like it means business.

The image below shows The Circle Coven altar set up. Sometimes practical concerns (such as the size of the table) dictates the placement of equipment more than tradition or personal preferences.

If you stand here, you are standing *in front* of the altar.

If you stand here, you are standing *behind* the altar.

Public or Large Group Rituals

Attending a public ritual is a wonderful way to meet other witches, learn about different branches of Paganism, expand your community network, and engage in magical experiences that simply aren't possible in solitary practice. However, it can be daunting to turn up at what may be an unfamiliar location to participate in a group activity where you don't have sole control. Whether you're attending your first public ritual or perhaps considering hosting one, here's my advice for doing it safely and successfully.

If you are planning to attend a public or group ritual, my first tip is that, in accordance with *PAN's Safety in the Circle* publication, you can leave a ritual at any time if you feel unsafe or threatened. I also suggest making sure that you centre yourself prior to the ritual, that you aren't intoxicated, and that you ground yourself when the ritual is finished.

There are a few other etiquette points I'd like to touch on for public rituals. Please respect the host/s of the ritual. Their practices may differ from yours, but they've done the hardyards by organising the ritual, so be kind, allow them some leeway, offer your help, and provide your support. They are likely to be under a lot of pressure, so try and withhold any well-meaning criticism or 'helpful tips' unless absolutely necessary.

Set your mobile phone to silent and unless you receive permission in advance, please don't take photographs during the ritual, particularly of people without their verbal, expressed approval. Some Pagans are not 'out of the broom closet', and sharing images might jeopardise their career or family connections.

Enjoy yourself and engage in what you are doing. Public and group rituals are fun and sometimes transformational. Allow yourself to embrace the magical aspects of a public ritual if these align with you. Introduce yourself to people, and listen to their stories. Try to not make assumptions based on physical appearance or clothing – you may get a surprise, as the Pagan community is dynamic and diverse.

On another note, I do not endorse people watching rituals, unless they are large, publicly held rituals, when it seems that pretty much anything is acceptable. In my opinion, witchcraft rituals are not a spectator sport. They are not held to amuse or entertain viewers or visitors or people who 'aren't sure about it' or 'want to see what it is about'. You are either inside the circle or you are far, far away. Perhaps you are taking a risk when you step into a ritual for the very first time. But daring to do new and uncertain things is a necessary part of life, and one we should continue to embrace regardless of our age or feelings of insecurity.

Walking the Wheel of the Year

By A'Rowan

The celebration of the eight sabbats is an acknowledgement of the cycles that occur in both our mundane and spiritual lives. The Wheel of the Year (WOTY) is depicted as a simple wheel with eight spokes dividing time, season and symbol. My personal understanding of the WOTY has evolved to a three-dimensional shape of a sphere that is centred by a star and the eight sabbats move and meld into each other, distinct but mutable, as above and below, and all contained in a glowing spinning ball.

You may like to visualise the WOTY as a spinning wheel or a circular component of a time piece that is in constant motion. Perhaps you have a circular garden bed where you can create your own living WOTY.

As we work with the WOTY concept, you will find your chosen depiction of the wheel will become your map. It is essential to have a starting point to understand and work with this ancient archetype for life and celebration. It will become both a guide and companion to your magical development. To begin though, there are a myriad of depictions available that focus on the southern hemisphere and appropriate dates for Australasian time zones. Choose your wheel and we will begin.

Your personal cycle

As your life progresses you become aware of a time of the year that you love, you feel empowered, is your lucky time or an annual end-time when a cyclic conclusion occurs. This awareness is accompanied by a physical and emotional connection that becomes part of our cyclic memory. We greet the return of this memory or knowing annually when we smell the jacaranda blossoms or feel the wind signal the change of season.

We have a personal responsibility to protect and nourish ourselves through these times for they are never neutral and always evolving. It is important that you become aware of the cycles that link your visual, physical and spiritual world.

You will experience these sabbats deeply through your rituals whether you practice as a solitary, are a member of a coven, or affiliated with a magical community. Myth and history will guide you and nature will humble you as you commit to the WOTY and all that it has to reveal.

Image by A'Rowan

Instructions for WOTY walking rituals

- Before you begin: what do you seek through this ritual? Any journey cycle will be linked to your personal cycle so align your needs and expectations.
- Choose your companions to walk with you, and you with them.
- Which deity and/or myth cycle will guide your progress? Choose from the pantheons of gods and goddesses, saints or ancestors.
- How do you map your journey? Write and draw in your Book of Shadows before and after the ritual, or during if you need to capture a significant insight.
- Narrate your own new story in homage and reverence for the natural cycles of change.
- Thank those who walked with you.

The WOTY is a landscape to be traversed, a concept that you make real by recognising the deeper aspects of the cycle. Sharpen your skills of navigation and orientation. Ways to do this are to select your guides and choose to follow or diverge; make your own cyclic journeys and acknowledgements; map your inner and outer landscape; plant your garden and live with a rich collection of souvenirs from your journey.

The sabbats are listed with the companion ritual. These are walking rituals if possible, where space is moved through and across to make the connection a psychomotor link as well as physical...so much more than walking...

Samhain: *Seek the Flame and Ask*
Your ritual could involve a journey to a memorial in a local park, or creating your own temple in your ritual area at home. You will need a central flame and quarters to work within your own temple. The flame may be a candle in your sacred space, or an image held in your heart for the duration of this ritual.

The Eternal Flame in the Anzac Square Memorial in Brisbane is an example of a public memorial to enact this rite. It is a gathering point to remember those who fought for our freedom, our warrior ancestors who sacrificed and made their own journey to long life in the otherworlds. The flame is central and continually burns with flickering energy. The temple that surrounds the flame is open to the sky and features columns that can be aligned with the quarters. The significant ritual aspects of this site are the circular temple and pillars that can be aligned, the flame and the space to walk around the boundary when required, always starting in the East.

Choose your time of day or evening, as this is a private ritual and you must feel safe while doing it.

Create your temple centred around the flame with the quarters identified.

Start in the East, then turn to face the South, then West and North, finally returning to the East.

The upper part of the flame, where it flickers and dissolves into the air, is your point of focus/contact. Abide a while and let yourself see if there are shapes or flickers of colour and light that seem to be there just for you. To seek and find even one small message or image or rhythm or colour is all that is needed. This ritual does not seek complex associations.

Ask what you will, but let your questions be contemplative and open ended. Focus on the flame and walk slowly around it, stopping at the quarters and breathing deeply as you move.

Remember to walk gently and to let the flame provide what you seek.

When you have finished your ritual, extinguish the flame without breath but with the gentle touch of gratitude and farewell.

Yule: *Ancestor Earth*

Possible locations include sandy cliff faces, garden rocks, or with your favourite opaque crystal. Kangaroo Point Cliffs in Queensland is one of my favourite places to undertake this ritual.

When walking past majestic cliffs, the layers of stratification can become a symbolic story of time captured in stone while observed with your witch's vision. The essentially horizontal formation and linear colours can be disrupted by cyclic changes, and you can identify fractures and upheavals that bring a beautiful discord to the rock face. Nothing needs to be perfect. These changes remind us that nature is a mirror of life, always changing and always surprising.

Your role here is one of witness and seeker, as you investigate the rock as if it is a treasure map or atlas. What patterns and rock formations do you follow? What textures and colours guide you? Move mindfully and use your sight/insight to connect with a part of the rock formation that resonates with your purpose of connection. Perhaps the recollection of a song and the favourite lines your loved ones sang, a photo of your ancestors as a direct connection through site specific associations, or the reverie of a dream will accompany you as you walk with the landscape.

Silently greet and warmly welcome your ancestor associations. Acknowledging can be a powerful way to rekindle your connection to ancestors both known and unknown, revealed in the colours and textures of the rock and silently communicated to you.

Rocks absorb the warmth of the sun during the day and radiates this heat in the evening to keep the soil and plants warm in the cool of the night. This ancient process of heat absorption and radiation suggests that this ritual is best done in the early evening (always safely). Hold the warmth of the rock as a promise of winter retreating and the new growth to come.

Bring a token memory to your home: a photograph, a small rock if one presents without damage, a sprinkle of sand.

Commit this reminder to your altar, print the image to display in your Book of Shadows and plan to do this walk again when next the wheel turns to Yule time.

Imbolc: *Flow Ritual*
Two bodies of water flowing beside each other represent peace and potential for transformation. The fertile strip that lies between the twin flowing waters is the rich ground for planting and waiting, for planning and reaping.

This ritual requires you work to with two bodies of water. Locate two rivers or creeks, two ocean inlets or prepare two ritual bowls of rainwater or purified water. The energy of moving water, of the flow, is significant as is it is bordered and contained by the quiet space on the banks of the water flow. This space in between and beside is your place for meditation, divination and positive introspection.

You can choose to start this ritual outdoors and conclude in your home or garden undisturbed.

The essence is in the sound of the water as it moves. This is your link – listen, record the sound, absorb the sound of the flow and carry this with you.

The visualization is of the body of water that needs to be crossed to reach the bank where there is a large fire burning. The glow from the fire lights your path across the water. The water can be as shallow as you wish. There is no struggle intended, just your journey across the water. As you move in the water, collect a small bowl or cup (or whatever you have) to carry water with you to the other side. Know that you are immersed in the flow of life and all is safe. Keep moving through.

When you reach the bank or the edge of the water, pour your container of water onto the earth. This ancient act honours your crossing by pouring a libation as a blessing for your journey so far and to honour the divinity of the water. This act of pouring is not to measure the spill, but to acknowledge our source.

Approach the light and warmth. Rest.

Did you feel the current as you crossed or was the water still? What washed away? Do you feel cleansed and welcome? Why were you wading? Were you called from the other side? Are your feet wet?

Ostara: *Queen of Spring*

This is a jacaranda blossom time ritual with a focus on how you are the Queen of your Realm. If there are no jacaranda flowers nearby, choose a different local bloom.

Personal power and collective power are celebrated by this ritual with the intention of acknowledging your sovereignty over the positive aspects of your world and mundane life.

Gather the flowers from a newly blossomed tree, preferably close to your home.

Make your crown and craft and fashion it to be a perfect fit. You can use any form of crown you like, and fresh flowers to decorate. Jacaranda flowers have a fragile and temporary beauty which is perfect for this ritual. The crown becomes an ephemeral symbol; work to create this. Capture in your muscle memory the weight of your crown, the lightness and scent of the flowers. Transform the real into a memory – your invisible crown that you wear always.

Wear your crown and royal regalia, dress yourself fully for you are Queen of your Realm.

This ritual involves wise counsel as the Queen is sought for her wisdom and foresight. Consider how wise you are to know, to find, to solve, and to create in your life. Seek audience with your inner Queen and know that she is there always.

In your ritual, transform your crown from fragile and temporary in this realm, to a perpetual diadem in your spiritual realm, your otherworld self.

Greet your queenly self each day, wear your invisible crown and claim sovereignty over your realm.

Beltane: *Beneath the Veil*
This ritual walks you towards love, union and reunion, self-discovery and self-empowerment. It can be practiced anywhere that is private, and you are required to be most humbly unadorned, skyclad if you can.

You require a bowl of rain or purified water and a ring or piece of jewellery that you always wear that is safe to immerse.

This is a gentle ritual that both pieces together a strong and renewed internal framework, and it starts bone deep.

Light your ritual space with candlelight, claim the quarters and immerse your chosen jewellery item in the water bowl placed in the centre of your ritual space. This now becomes your ritual bath, pond or ocean, even a sacred lake.

Visualise a mound of old bones, delicate and fragile, stacked at your feet. These are the bones of your old self and your quest is to bathe and reassemble these into your new structure. You are cleansing and re-establishing a new inner strength that is marrow deep. Take each bone and hold it as gently as you would something old and precious. Wash your bones and visualize the melding of these loved and renewed bones back into your body. They are your base strength and the start of all growth. These bones can symbolise your creative plans and love magick.

You will hold your bones as gently as you would something old and precious, but also young and strong with potential.

You are trusted to hold and supported as you complete this task.

This is time for healing and trust, self-focused love magick and making new again our essential structure. Renewal of our bones occurs every seven years, so keep track of this annual inner build and use the time to focus on bone health with each turn of the wheel.

This is a ritual for clear seeing, the thin veil allowing an inner and outer focus as you put your pieces back together. Conclude by placing your jewellery back on your body and casting the ritual water to your garden.

Litha: *Sister River*

The feminine aspects of mother and female deity are celebrated here with walking beside a body of moving water as an essential requirement. The contemplative aspect could be the vastness contained by the banks of the river and the beginning and end flow of the water into the ocean. The river is permeable, transient and immutable in its presence. You can find it, follow it, swim and journey in this space. You can walk it or in your dream state you can conjure it.

The annual journey upstream is ancient, moving against the flow, purposefully. You know the feeling of straining against the current – your efforts are doubled and you doubt your commitment, but have a purpose as fundamental and driven as the stars who watch your journey. You move up the river as a fully accomplished entity, wise and full. You have much to share, much to birth, much to contribute to this cyclic turning of the wheel.

Your river journey is a pathway to your place of rest. There is no death here, just a release of your potential/learning/teaching. Here you share time, words, gestures, unspoken deeds, birthing ideas while rebirthing yourself.

The purpose of your upriver journey is to let go and release. Sharing is always the intent: letting your ideas and wisdom flow down the river where they blissfully move towards the place where they are needed and stored.

I create small tokens, crystal gifts and messages of greeting that I gift to my future self, to be opened next year when the wheel has turned full cycle. Upon rediscovering these gifts, I am reminded that the passing of time is marked by learning and releasing.

The cycle starts again when next the wheel turns and there will be a return of the next special ones who will swim upstream to be embraced by you.

You must remember that you were never alone.

Lughnasadh: *Rain and Light*

This ritual is a cleansing preparation for this turning of the wheel. The gift of rain literally falls from the sky, and it is your opportunity to bathe fully in the mystery of connection between your outer and inner worlds.

Prepare for this ritual by planning what you will require, for the rain comes when it will.

This ritual is best done in private, in your own outdoor space or safe place. The ritual asks that you allow part of your body to become wet by the downpour.

I like to start with my hands cupped to collect the precious drops and to mark an invisible pentagram in front of me to walk into. You may wish to only immerse your hands or if your situation permits, allow your head to become dampened and then more of your body.

For urban witches, this can be walked along your street, just for a short while to let the edge of your body be touched by the rain and absorb it into your aura.

You are aiming to energise the intersection of you and the atmosphere with points of pure light. The visualisation of rain becoming a soft silken glow on your skin can be enhanced by gently tapping your skin with your damp finger tips, awakening and energising. The symbolic immersion and marriage of outer and inner worlds is celebrated here. This consequent glow can be taken inside your home and shared.

A small bowl of this rainwater can be collected and kept on your altar, shared with your animals and plants or loved ones.

Mabon: *Harvest Cake*

The alchemical and transmuting experience of combining ingredients is at the heart of this harvest rite.

This ritual starts in your kitchen, at your hearth. You require a recipe that is borrowed, preferably from an ancestor, to make this harvest cake. The recipe may be for any cake, as long as you ensure that the cake will symbolise the bounty of the fruits of your harvest, possibly even using your own, a loved one's or community produce.

Ritualise the ingredients, and cleanse in purified water any items that require washing. Use new or unopened ingredients and focus on the properties of the ingredients. Where have they travelled from to be with you; thank them for their journey so far.

The combining of ingredients can be slow and deliberate, speak your wishes to the mix while your oven warms. Your athame can be your companion for this ritual, laying protectively near you while you prepare your 'potion'.

Document any changes you make to the recipe. This can be committed to your Book of Shadows for the ingredients may require review, reflection and sharing.

When your harvest cake making is complete and as it cools, this is a time to relax. Later, enjoy your cake with homemade honey mead or as part of 'cakes and ale' in your coven ritual. Store extra harvest cake in the freezer; seal it into a container that is marked with your magical name or protective pentagram. You can eat and share when required.

Your harvest cake celebrates the completion of this growing cycle as part of the turning of the wheel. Nourish the land with food and drink and, like Hansel and Gretel, leave a trail or sprinkling of cake crumbs for those in need. This trail does not lead to you, but by creating it in your garden, along the edge of the footpath, you ensure a cyclic nourishment for those who follow.

You have shared your harvest and now rest, for the place that you seek, you are already there.

FOCUS: Magick and Spellwork

Here's the bit you have all been waiting for: spellwork! These next pages contain information about different forms of magick, and how to craft a spell. I've also provided a few examples of spells you may like to try.

Magick – Tips and Techniques

Magick is intrinsically associated with witchcraft. By the way, we spell the word magick with a 'k', on the advice of Aleister Crowley, who did this to differentiate the occult from card tricks or stage magic. He also provides us with one of the better-known definitions of magick (in *Magick Book IV Liber ABA*):

'Magick is the science and art of causing change to occur in conformity with will.'

In other words, magick is deliberately making something happen via an altered state of consciousness with minimal physical means. We, as witches, enact magick by accessing a source of power or energy (such as the gods, ancestors, elements or indescribable cosmic forces) and then focussing our will towards an aim. Every person has the ability to connect with 'magical power', however they choose to describe it.

The goals of magick include the improvement of our lives, the transformation of ourselves and mystical attainment. This is also known as the Great Work.

One key principle behind our ability to create change through magick is the occult precept of 'as above, so below'. The macrocosm (the bigger scheme of things) effects and can be affected by the microcosm (i.e., us as humans). Every event occurring on the physical/material level occurs first in the intangible, less dense dimensions of the astral, mental or spiritual planes.

To sum up, thoughts are things, or more correctly, thoughts can become things. Having said that, there are many factors influencing future events in our lives which we simply cannot change as they are pre-destined or fated for ourselves or others. We don't always get exactly what we ask for or desire. Sometimes we get what we need, rather than what we think we want.

Magick and spellwork tips

While I enjoy arcane poetry and veiled illusions, I also treasure a bit of straight talk. Here's some of my hot tips about magick and spellwork:

+ There are consequences to *every* action we take. Sometimes we can anticipate the consequences from our magical workings. Other times we are completely blindsided by the results. Try to consider all potential consequences before starting a spell working. Meditate on it. Perform a divination. Go to sleep, and decide the next day. This often means that I don't end up doing any spellwork to attempt to magically change the situation because I realise that things are as they should be, there are good reasons for that, and I need to accept matters for what they are. Doing nothing is a valid magical action.

+ A spell is simply a recipe to help you achieve a magical outcome. The energy flowing through you is the catalyst and you are creator. You are the most important part of any spellwork.

+ If appropriate, consider the free will of others in your spellwork, and the potential impacts that your spell could have upon the person. Is your neighbour annoying you? Are you thinking of putting together a nice little curse to 'get back at them'? Ask yourself whether you really know everything about the situation and if there is an alternative option.

+ Every conscious and deliberate action is a magical action. You don't need to burn incense, create witchtok videos or hoard shiny crystals to be magical. Consider your true will, harness your heartfelt desires and focus.

+ Unless there is a change of consciousness (away from the everyday, monkey mind brain) it's unlikely you will achieve an effective magical outcome.

+ Look for evidence that your spellcraft has been effective. But don't obsess over whether or not your spell worked, as this can dilute the spell and render it useless. Measure, reflect and diarise.

+ Fix things in the physical realm as much as possible before and/or after doing spellwork to improve the matter. Don't use magick to avoid actions or remedies in the mundane world. Always consider what practical changes you will make in alignment with the associated spellwork.

+ Try to be better. Do things to make the world better place. Act locally but think globally – or Universally.

+ Be kind to yourself. Sometimes you need to take a break from magical stuff and read a trashy novel, go shoe shopping, or eat some hot chips with tomato sauce (or gravy if that's your thing). No-one is judging here. Balance is vital. Don't burn out, as you simply can't be perfect all the time.

Magical power

Magical energy or power is everywhere around and within us. However, the source we are most aware of and connected to is our *personal power*. Our levels can ebb and rise frequently – sometimes rapidly when we experience heightened emotions, such as delight or fury. It can be easy to temporarily deplete our store of personal energy due to the demands of busy, modern day life, and feel drained and exhausted. Also, people colloquially known as psychic vampires, can deplete our personal energy levels. Everyone has had the experience of walking away from a super-negative, energy-sapping person and feeling utterly and grimly miserable afterwards.

Personal power is *not* the ideal source to access when performing magick, unless you have the skill to continuously replenish or 'top up' your supply. Visualise a goblet full of glowing golden liquid. From above, a never-ending stream of radiant liquid is poured into the goblet, and because of the high level of fluid already within, the excess runs over the edge of the goblet and seeps into the earth to be transformed. This is the ideal situation. Using too much personal power during ritual or spellwork is akin to tipping over that goblet, where all the contents spill onto the ground and the fluid within the goblet can't be replenished.

To keep your personal power charged and maintained at a comfortable level, create physical and emotional boundaries for safety and harmony. You also need to eat healthy food, drink adequate fluids and try to avoid substances which are harmful to your body. As well as looking after the physical side of things, tend to your emotional and spiritual gardens. For some practical ways to do this, refer to the *Bringing Magick into Everyday Life* chapter.

Here are some seemingly limitless sources of energy, as alternatives to personal power:

- ✦ **Earth** energies which pulse through all manifestations of nature's realm. Sometimes it's difficult to feel or access these in the middle of a busy city, but deep down, Earth energy is always present. Stand with bare feet upon the earth to revitalise and heal.
- ✦ **Air, Fire or Water** elemental energies. You may find that it is easier to connect to some elemental energies, in comparison to others. This could be due to your personality, past experiences or astrological makeup.

- ✦ **Star power** hrough tapping into the dance of the cosmos. Become aware of the planets of our solar system, the sun, stars and moon. Just spending a couple of minutes in the direct, warming rays of the sun can provide a boost. Stand outside on the night of the full moon and embrace the gentle energies.
- ✦ **Divine energy** by accessing the numinous, the Universe, the Gods, that sense of the something greater, grander and wiser than yourself brings an immense charge of energy.

Raising Energy with Sound and Movement

By Merewyn

Scriptures worldwide express the idea that the first cosmic manifestation was vibration, whether sound, light or breath. This primal vibration, differentiating into sounds, colours or rhythmic breathing formed the basis for all that followed.

Sacred music and dance are powerful tools that have been used by cultures throughout the ages to awaken consciousness, call in power, heal the body and spirit and enhance the celebration of important occasions. In both modern and ancient times, dance and music are considered not just for entertainment but as forms of active prayer and worship, a way of communing with the gods and goddesses, of re-connecting with the cycles of nature and with all life, of producing an altered state of consciousness.

Energy raising is something anyone and everyone can do. It only takes a little practice, the ability to let go, and the willingness to at least try. You don't need to play an instrument; you don't need to be able to sing. There is a saying in Zimbabwe:

'If you can walk, you can dance; if you can talk, you can sing.'

Chanting

Chanting is an ancient and universal practice, usually done in accompaniment with drumming, handclapping, rattles and sometimes other musical instruments. It can generate the energetic build-up needed to increase psychic power to an intense level. This is especially true when chanting is done within a group. Sometimes the excitement builds so high that frenzied states of consciousness occur.

Ancient Greeks such as Plato and Aristotle recognized that the healing power of music was grounded in its relation to the mathematical structure of the cosmos and humanity. In ancient Greece, sorcerers howled their chants; early medieval magicians sang their chants in forceful voices. The Gregorian chant sung by Benedictine monks uses the middle to higher frequencies of the human voice to energize the body and promote mental and spiritual activity.

A chant usually consists of only a few words and a simple melody that can be easily learned and readily repeated. Because of their repetitive quality, chants put you quickly into a meditative state and help to clear and centre our minds. A chant is designed to activate and balance the inner self, to amplify and raise energy and focus spiritual power. As we chant the words and melody repetitively, we give voice to our feelings, deepen our devotion, and call forth what we want into our lives.

Every chant has a specific purpose and meaning that can be invoked each time it is sung. A chant accumulates power with each repetition. It helps us to focus our concentration; to quiet and empty our active thinking minds and connect deeply with the core of our being. The simpler and more repetitive the chant, the more effective it is. Repetition puts us easily in a hypnotic state where we no longer have to think about what we are singing; the chant begins to work through us. We are no longer doing the singing; the singing is being us.

A chant should be repeated over and over, either aloud or silently, to help attune to a particular vibration, deity or energy you want to bring into your life. An effective chant can stay with you and reverberate in your mind throughout the day. It can increase balance and harmony and create a deep trance state which can last for hours.

Through chants and songs, we plant positive thoughts and ideas which are then quickly made emotional through music. The feelings evoked by music magnifies words. Psychologists have found that music works much faster than affirmations, or the spoken word alone, for programming our subconscious. As we chant, we sharpen our focus and intention. When a group makes sounds or music together, a vibrational force field is created which accelerates and intensifies the magical process.

As you sing, it is good to attune to the essential quality and power of the chant, to feel its unique spirit and vibration. Some chants work best if sung in a strong steady, sustained voice all the way through. Others need to be sung slowly; still others more quickly. Many start slowly and quietly, increasing in speed and sound as the energy builds. Whenever your mind wanders, especially when doing a repetitive mantra, come back to the feeling. Let the feeling deepen – and so the energy builds. Let the hum expand and move through you, waking up any parts of your body that are asleep or resistant. Feel as if you are giving yourself an internal sound massage. Feel the energy building in your body, feel it being projected around the circle, and feel it as it reaches a peak until it is ready to be released.

Chant with your heart open, and mind alert. Chant with gleeful Spirit. Feel the vibration throughout your body. Notice how it transforms your state of being.

Studies have shown that vibrations from rhythmic sounds have a profound effect on brain activity. In shamanic traditions, drums are used to transport listeners into other realms of reality. The vibrations from the constant rhythm affect the brain in a way that allows the listeners to achieve an altered state of mind and journey out of their body.

Brain pattern studies show that the steady rhythmic beat of a drum struck four and a half times per second is the key to transporting a person into the deepest part of their consciousness. It is no coincidence that 4.5 beats, or cycles per second corresponds to the trance like state of Theta brain wave activity. In direct correlation, we see similar effects brought on by the constant and rhythmic drone of Tibetan Buddhist chants, which transport the listeners into realms of blissful meditation.

Toning

Toning is extending or prolonging the vocal sounds of each vowel of a spoken word. Toning does not include a melody – just the sound of the vibrating breath. It is a simple yet powerful technique, accessible to everyone regardless of musical ability or training. Through toning you can immediately experience the beneficial effects of sound on your physical, mental, emotional, and spiritual wellbeing.

Toning is not singing and there's no aesthetic judgement involved. The sound you make does not have to be pretty; the point of toning is not the quality of the sound but your experience of the vibration and its results. Listen with your whole being, and be open to the total effect of the sound. Link your voice, breath, and awareness together to enhance your appreciation of your own true power in life.

Meditative toning appears to massage body and mind from the inside out. It can help you focus and relax; release negative emotions; reduce stress; and improve stamina and concentration. Toning synchronizes the brainwaves and helps relieve tension within a few minutes. It can help you awaken and strengthen your sense of self and align you to the deepest vibrations of soul and spirit.

Musical instruments in ritual

Keep the musical accompaniment simple: the simpler the better. A strong drumbeat or rattle shake that accentuates the natural rhythm of the chant works best. Add other easy-to-use instruments such as percussion and bells. Let the power of the chant or song be foremost. Chants are often more powerful when they are sung unaccompanied.

Drumming is one of the most ancient and powerful ways to accompany chants, dances and ritual. The drum is round; it is a feminine form which awakens our instinctual earthy nature as well as ancient images and symbols. The drum is used to carry and sustain the energy, to keep the inner pulse; it echoes the heartbeat of Mother Earth and of all life.

In ritual, the drummer needs to be able to keep a steady even beat and be sensitive to the energy of the group process. They need to know how to listen and follow the group pulse, in order to support what is happening, rather than becoming a distraction. This is not the place for fancy drum rhythms, improvisation, and solo acts. If the basic heartbeat stops, the energy will drop immediately. At certain times, this may be what is required within the ritual. At other times, it may be appropriate to gradually speed up the tempo to raise the energy, or to slow it down to ground the energy.

Rattles and shakers, like the drum, are powerful ritual tools. Dried gourds are often used. When rattles are shaken, the seeds are brought to life. The gourds may be decorated with your personal symbols of power. Alternatively, you can make your own shakers by putting a few seeds, dried peas, or even small crystals into vessels such as a glass jar, pewter flask or even a plastic bottle.

The rattling sound of the gourd is thought to open the doorway into the spirit world, to call our spirit guides, allies and guardians to us. Rattles are also used to heighten our intention, to focus and direct energy. You can rattle to create sacred space or to send healing energy into a sick person's body. When you shake the rattle up and down, you call in active masculine energy; when you shake it side-to-side you invoke receptive, feminine energy.

Jingle bells, or sleigh bells, are hand-held pieces of wood with bells or small cymbals attached. They give a wonderful chinging sound when shaken rhythmically. These instruments are readily available or quite easy to make at home.

Clapping sticks can be used effectively to beat out a simple rhythm and connect us to the earth. The rhythm can be of your choosing. As you focus on what you are doing and what you are feeling, clap the sticks together however you like. As you get further into the rhythm, you may change the beat slightly to *feel* it more, be open to how it feels, be drawn in, become one with it. You can also use your hands and body as a percussion instrument – clap your hands together, or against your body. Your stamping feet can also add a strong rhythmic foundation to your dancing and chanting.

Spellwork Step-by-Step

For those who like checklists, here's one to get you started in spell casting.

Prepare
1. Decide on the results you want. Be clear about your planned intentions and goal. Write these out when you are 100% certain of what you want to achieve.
2. Ensure your magical working is justified in accordance with your own ethical system. Consider all potential consequences. You may like to ask your guides /higher-self/deity for 'permission' or agreement through a divinatory reading or deep meditation.
3. Determine the date and timing for your spellwork. Choose the correct moon phase and day of the week, according to need. See the *The Magic of Time* chapter for suggestions. However, if a time feels overwhelmingly 'right' despite everything else, go for it!
4. Gather your ingredients. Substitute if necessary. Plan ahead regarding how you will dispose of the ingredients at the end of your working.
5. Prepare the physical environment. Position candles safely, add the necessary items or equipment to your altar.
6. Ensure you will not be disturbed by phone, pets or people.
7. Prepare yourself by abstaining from food/chemicals/drama, as needed. The intensity of the spell working will dictate what's required.
8. Do a pre-ritual cleanse (see suggestions in *Preparing for ritual* section) and dress in specially chosen clothing and jewellery.
9. Think of your purpose continually, in a dreamlike, relaxed state.
10. Perform an aura cleansing or centering activity immediately before the ritual.

Craft
1. Focus wholly and soley on your magical working, and what you want to achieve. Let nothing else – especially doubt – enter your mind. This is essential.

2. Create the conditions to enter an altered state of consciousness. Options include chanting, drumming, rhythm, movement or meditation.
3. Create what you want to happen in your mind. Visualise it as if you are doing or acheiving something, not wanting something. In other words, focus on the end result, not the process.
4. When the image or concept is clear to you and held very firmly within your being, this is when you *send* energy – which can be raised by a group, or by yourself – towards it (or the spell ingredients). This can feel like a forcing, *pushing* sensation, followed by a sense of *release* and completion. The feeling of completion will signal that you have done all you can at this stage.
5. After achieving the state of release, you should feel calm and still. If you feel emotional or anxious, or if you've felt nothing, you may not have completed the spell properly. Either try again, or abandon what you are doing and attempt it another time.

Complete
1. Pay your respects and/or give thanks to your Gods, guides or allies.
2. Close and clear your physical area.
3. Ground yourself by eating or drinking.
4. Write in your ritual diary.
5. Do what you need to assist the magical working, for example, sending the resume, buying the lottery ticket, making the phone call.
6. After the ritual, *do not continue to focus on your spell.* Yep, forget all about it. Don't dwell on your working. Keep silent; don't discuss it with others or continue to post on social media. Releasing the energy and allowing it to do its work is an essential part of spellwork. Let it go!

Results vary.
Small projects may manifest within 24 hours; larger projects can take several months to begin and several years to manifest. Repetition and perseverance help.

Colour Correspondences

The following list of colour correspondences can be applied to any spell working. If in doubt, or if you can't locate a specific colour, simply use white as it contains the spectrum of all colours within it. Colour symbolism can easily be incorporated into magical workings through candles, fabric, cords, ribbon, paper, ink, or paint.

There are many lists of colour correspondences available. There is no one definitive list, as practitioners and groups have varying reasons behind their choices, so don't get too worried about the fine print. Experiment, reflect, and discover your personal preferences.

Black (or grey): cursing, reversing, uncrossing, binding or removing bindings; discord, repelling or releasing; stopping gossip or lies.
Blue: truth, inspiration, protection, peace, patience; healing; the Blue Ray.
Brown: Earth energies; attracts material possessions and solid financial success; animals; finding lost objects; the home.
Green: prosperity and abundance; fertility; healing and health; good luck; new beginnings; success; Goddess.
Orange: change a current situation; powerful fluidity and flexibility.
Pink: love of an affectionate nature; romance; friendship; femininity; pleasant dreams; harmony in the home.
Purple (dark): government and legal systems; protection from the unknown; deeply held secrets.
Purple: psychic ability; protection; break bad luck; divination.
Red: love and sex; vitality, strength and passion; a great booster to improve physical health when feeling tired and run down.
White: can be used instead of other colours; a general all round 'vitamin pill' – protection, peace, spirituality, attainments in life, truth; powers of a higher nature; wholeness; spiritual strength; lunar energy; healing; consecration.
Yellow: intellect, study, imagination, creativity, confidence, action; great for work-related issues.

Candle Magick

Fire is an integral aspect of magical practice. As candles are cheap and easily available, they are perfect to use in spellwork and rituals. The flame of a candle can represent our highest ideals, while the smoke appears to move between worlds and bear subtle messages. The candle itself reminds us of the physical realm and the principles of transformation as the melted wax drips or disappears.

Beeswax candles are the most environmentally friendly candles, although vegans generally will steer clear of them. Vegetable oil (such as soy or coconut) candles are ecologically better than candles made from paraffin. Paraffin candles may release toxic chemicals, so are best avoided. Most cheap tealight candles are made from paraffin, and as a double whammy, the metal cannister of tealight candles adds to the landfill burden. At home, I prefer to use a reusable, wicked lamp. Some lamps work well with vegetable oil bought from the supermarket, which is a bonus.

Here are some tips for candle magick:

- Safety first. Make sure there are no billowing curtains, robe sleeves or flammable materials nearby. If a candle is left to burn overnight, I suggest relocating it to your bathtub or shower recess. Keep lit candles away from animals and children.
- You may like to create a symbol or design which encapsulates your intentions. Carve this into the candle; or write on a piece of paper, and wrap it around the candle or put the paper in front of the candle. Be careful if you wrap paper around a candle, as it will catch alight when the candle burns to that level, which could be disastrous if you haven't prepared a firesafe space.
- Put photographs, marriage certificates, and other items you don't want to damage, in front of candles as part of your spellwork.
- Dried herbs or personal body items can be blended into the wax. An easy way to do this is burn a candle for a short period of time until the wax

becomes soft or liquid, then add your items to the melted wax. Wait for it to harden again, then relight to complete your spell.
- ✦ Snuff candles. Do not blow them out. This is a way to pay respect to the Fire elementals which accompanied you during your spellwork.
- ✦ Dispose of remnants in environmentally friendly and appropriately elemental ways:
    - Bury in the soil (Earth)
    - Scatter to the winds (Air)
    - Combust (Fire), then mix the ashes with compost and bury
    - Mix with water and soluble plant fertiliser to feed plants; flush non-toxic fluids down a drain or release into a stream (Water)
    - For destructive magick, put the leftover items in a compostable bag, add a piece of fruit and a small crystal and bury. Sometimes, I simply place the remains straight into the wheely bin. Good riddance to bad rubbish.

Dressing a candle

Before using a taper or pillar candle in a ritual or working, first anoint the candle with oil and energise it. This is called dressing a candle. It creates a link between you and the candle and your declared intentions.

Place a small amount of the chosen oil on your hands and rub them together until they slide easily and tingle. Face in the direction which best suits your magical needs; refer to the *Correspondences* chapter if you would like a refresher. Hold the candle in your palms, with one hand grasping the top half of the candle, and the other hand grasping the bottom half.

Visualise glowing energy entering your body via your feet and crown chakra, flowing through your body and into the palms of your hands. Feel them grow warm with energy, and visualise that energy moving into the candle. Move your hands up and down the candle, with the oil allowing your hands to slide easily. When the candle is properly energised, you will feel an inner sense of peace and calm.

To test the effectiveness of your candle dressing, use a pendulum. Place your charged candle a short distance away from an undressed candle. Hold the pendulum over the top of the charged candle and observe how it swings. Now hold it over the top of the uncharged candle. Usually, pendulums swing far more vigorously when held over a properly dressed candle.

Miscellaneous candle magick information

+ ***Relighting a candle.*** In general, do not relight a candle which has gone out by itself. Either your magick is concluded or you have not performed the spell properly. However, it's fine to relight a candle which has been deliberately snuffed. If you plan to use a large, slow-burning candle on multiple occasions, mark it with a line, or poke a needle into the wax, to pre-plan when you will snuff the candle.
+ ***Re-using candles.*** Yes, you can do this, but it depends on what the candle was previously used for, and the anticipated working. If both purposes are similar, I feel it's OK.
+ ***Old, broken candles.*** In general, do not use a candle which has been broken into pieces for a new spell. However, you may like to upcycle the pieces of wax to create a new candle.
+ ***Double-wick candles.*** Burn to create confusion or to delay a situation.

Spell Bottles

Spell bottles have been used for centuries. Old bottles are still being found sealed up in the walls and foundations of historical houses. Usually, the vessels are made of glass or ceramic, and have been filled with hair, nails and fluid such as urine.

Spell bottles are wonderful magical items, as they are a tangible reminder of your spell. You can place spell bottles in prominent positions, such as on the windowsill, a bathroom shelf or beside a dog kennel, and non-witches might only guess at the purpose. A pretty, coloured spell bottle can be easily disguised as vessel for gourmet oil or bath salts. Alternatively, bury your spell bottle, hide it under the front steps, or seal it within your house walls if you are renovating.

In principle, if the bottle remains intact or unbroken it will retain its potency. However, you might prefer to refresh the ingredients once a year.

House protection spell bottle

You will need:
- One glass jar with a lid
- Three generous scoops of salt
- Three cloves of garlic
- Nine bay leaves
- Eight basil leaves – or eight pinches of dried basil
- Four pinches of black pepper
- Fluids to fill the bottle, such as water, oil or alcohol (or just include the dry ingredients if preferred)
- Paper and pen
- One bowl.

Craft:

Carefully choose the most auspicious time, for example, a bright and sunny Friday. Assemble all ingredients. One by one, add each dry ingredient to the bowl, saying;

"May the power of [ingredient name] *shield and protect my home and all within it."*

If you like, write these words, or the words from the chant below onto the piece of paper, and add this into the bowl.

Mix together all dry items with your hands. Visualise your home as a shining, safe, guarded, secure place of sanctuary. Here's a chant by Melissa you may like to say:

Magick from the Goddess bring,
Protection from all nasty things.
Protect me, my home and all my kin,
May peace and love dwell within.
Guard against harm and enmity,
This is my will, so mote it be!

Pour the mixture into the jar. Add fluid if you wish. Seal tightly and place in the desired location while saying the following words: *"It shall be done."*

Money spell bottle

You will need:
- Eight coins (the denomination or value doesn't matter)
- Eight kernels of dried corn
- Eight bay leaves (or local gum leaves)
- Eight kernels of dried wheat or pinches of wheat flour
- Eight sesame seeds
- Eight small smooth stones, green or white in colour
- Eight nuts, such as macadamias or walnuts
- A drop of patchouli or fragrant oil
- A suitable bottle or container.

Craft:
Place all ingredients into a suitable vessel and cap it tightly. Shake the bottle gently for eight minutes, charging it with energy while chanting:

> *"Grain, bring gain. Money bring wealth. Herbs make it grow. Stones let it stay."*

Place the money spell bottle on a green cloth in a visible location. As often as possible, leave your purse or wallet or credit cards nearby. Allow money to come into your life and remain with you.

Spell Boxes

Spell boxes work by merging and mixing the energies trapped within their confines. When the spell is done, the contained and concentrated energies are then released to work in accordance with the magical goal. To create a spell box, choose a wooden box with a firm fitting lid. It doesn't have to be enormous – mine is 10 cm by 10cm. A box with a little lock or padlock is ideal.

Some people prefer to use a different box for each spell. If workings have a positive intention, I usually reuse the same box, and have had no ill results from doing this.

To prepare the box for your spellwork, raise the lid on the night of a full moon. As you hold the box towards each of the cardinal directions, say:

"*By the Powers of Air* [then Fire/Water/Earth while facing the associated directions] *I dedicate this spell box to the working of magic. You are now a tool of transformation.*"

When the box is not in use, wrap in a natural fabric cloth and store out of sight.

Love spell box

This spell is designed to attract a non-specific person into your life.

You will need:
- Your spell box
- One pink candle in a candle holder – large enough to be re-lit and burn over nine sessions
- Lighter or matches
- A piece of pink paper and a pen
- Dried rose petals – usually the petals from two roses is enough, although it depends on the size of your spell box
- Dried lavender flowers, a small handful
- Two rose quartz stones
- Two new finger rings, preferably made of silver or copper.

Craft:
Cut the paper into a heart shape. Draw or write your intentions onto it, such as the words *'genuine, nourishing love for me'*. Place the paper into the spell box.

One by one, hold the other ingredients (rose petals, lavender flowers, rings, stones) in your hands, and feel the joy and beauty of love fill you. Imbue these energies into the ingredients. Say: *"Symbol of love, bring love to me."*

One by one, place the ingredients into the spell box.

Light the candle and place it in front of the open box, which now contains all ingredients. Let the candle burn for nine minutes, then firmly close the lid of the spell box and quench the flame.

For the next eight nights, relight the candle, place it in front of the spell box and then open the lid. Again, focus all your energies on feeling the sensation of love radiating from you into the box. Do this for nine minutes, then close the lid and extinguish the candle.

On the tenth and final night, light the candle, but don't open the box. Say these or similar words:

"Petals, stones and ring,
Love you shall bring.
Out you go,
True love will flow.
So mote it be!"

Then open the lid of your spell box and sense the energies rushing out and spiralling into the aether to bring your love into manifestation. Snuff the candle.

Remove all the ingredients. Tie the two rings together with a pink or white ribbon and leave on your altar, or wrap in a piece of cloth and store them safely. Bury the other ingredients in a pot plant or garden bed, and if possible, plant lavender or a lovely herb on top.

Charm Bags

A charm bag, also known as a spell bag, is a small pocket of coloured material which is filled with charged items then closed with string or cord. Charm bags can be worn by a person or left in a specific location to attract or dispel certain influences.

There should always be an *odd* number of ingredients in a charm bag, and I like to include salt in every bag. The ingredients themselves will vary, depending on what you want to achieve, but can include herbs, crystals, powder, stones or feathers. If you want to personalise your working, include items such as hair, nail clippings, soiled clothing or used tissues.

While red is the go-to colour for charm bags, you can choose a colour fabric in keeping with the kind of spellwork to be undertaken. Draw or embroider appropriate sigils, runes, symbols or add decorations to the material if you wish. Make sure the cloth is made from tightly woven material, otherwise the powdery ingredients will seep through. You can use pre-made square or rectangular drawstring bags, or do what the coven usually does, which is cut round pieces of cloth approximately 20 cm in diameter. At the end of the working, tie the charm bag firmly closed with a piece of cord or ribbon.

Quick guide to creating a charm bag

- Make or acquire your bag or cloth. Choose the cord/string/twine to seal it closed.
- Hold each ingredient, one at a time. Say aloud the purpose of each item, before placing it into the bag or onto the cloth. For example, *"This rose quartz crystal will help fill my heart with love."*
- When all ingredients have been added, energetically charge the items by chanting or directing energy towards them.
- Seal your bag (tie a good strong knot!) and anoint it with an appropriate oil.
- The user wears the bag on them, next to their skin, for at least three to

seven days. For women with an ample bust, the charm bag can be tucked inside your bra. Alternatively, leave the cord long so the bag can be worn around the neck.

✦ After that, place the bag in a specific location. I've found tying charm bags to the bedframe under the mattress is a convenient place for health or wellbeing spells.

✦ On the same day, once a week, or once a month, anoint the bag with the oil used when the charm bag was created.

✦ Charm bags can work their magick for years! However, when you feel the bag's purpose has been completed, cut open the bag, and release the components appropriately by burning or burying. Do not reuse any of the contents of a charm bag, as the work has now been done.

Amulets and Talismans

Amulets
An amulet is a protective object which deflects negative energies or links to positive energies. It is usually a simple, naturally found object, such as a stone with a hole through it (a 'hag stone' or 'witches stone') or a four-leaf clover. Pretty much anything can serve as an amulet (such as a hairbrush, soup spoon or feather) as long as you believe it fits that purpose.

Amulets do not need to be made of 100% natural materials – just go with your personal preference. A Mediterranean 'eye' painted onto bright blue glass is a good example of a commonly used amulet. Old horseshoes are another time-honoured amulet, though opinions vary as to whether they should be placed upright or downwards over a doorway. European legend has it that iron horseshoes kept witches (or the fae) away, but practical experience shows this doesn't work as well in modern times.

If you engrave and consecrate an amulet it becomes a talismanic amulet.

Talismans
Talismans are human-made or deliberately altered objects which are then ritually charged. They can be used for many purposes, such as attracting a specific force or energy, or to deflect negative influences. The most powerful talismans are those made by the person who needs them, because of the enhanced magical links.

Quick guide to creating a talisman:
1. A talisman can be made of virtually any material, but it's best to choose a substance which corresponds to the desired use. Commonly used materials include parchment, paper, silver, copper, lead, glass or stone. You may need to form the item into a suitable size or shape before use.
2. Determine the appropriate weekday, hour and astrological timing.
3. Personalise the talisman by adding name and date of birth. Using an alternative alphabet such as Theban seems to work better than the usual English alphabet.

4. Inscribe with appropriate symbols such as:
   - A single rune or combine multiple runes to create a bind-rune.
   - A sigil. Create your own by transforming letters into a shape. Write down your goal into simple words. Cross out the letters that repeat, until you are left with a few letters. Then use your creativity to draw a symbol integrating those letters.
5. Focus clearly on your intentions as you physically create the talisman.
6. Consecrate the talisman. Read the *Consecration Ritual* chapter to learn how to do this.
7. Wear the talisman or put it in the required location.
8. Stay silent about your working.

A covener had the fantastic idea of using a blank, round dog tag as her talismanic item. It was the perfect size and shape. After it was inscribed, consecrated and charged, it easily attached to a chain.

Sweetening-up Spell

Honey jar (or sugar jar) spells originally came from Hoodoo traditions, but are now used by a range of practitioners. This sweetening-up method focuses on improving relationships rather than taking a binding or blocking approach. Honey jar spells can be used to help change negative opinions into positive ones, or encourage happier situations.

Here's a modified version of a honey jar spell. The best timing would be during a waxing or full moon.

You will need:
- Honey – vegans may like to substitute golden syrup, molasses or treacle
- Sugar
- Paper and pen
- A glass jar with a lid able to form a strong seal – make sure the jar is squeaky clean
- Optional – herbs, small crystals and flowers of choice.

Please note the amounts will vary depending on the size of the jar, so be flexible and creative.

Craft:
Half fill the jar with honey or syrup.

Write a short description of the situation that you want to sweeten. Write this down nine times on one side of the paper.

Fold over the paper once, keeping the writing on the inside. On one side, write your name in the centre. Also write key words to describe the positive interactions, for example, *happy, good job interview, great relationship, kind to me, promote love.*

Fold over the paper again, so the writing is on the inside. Decorate both sides of the folded paper with images, such as circles, stars, patterns, pentagrams or sigils.

Place the paper into the jar, which you have already half filled.

Add your herbs, crystals or other items to the jar.

Pour in the sugar saying:
"Sweetness keep and sweetness be."

Top up the jar with the rest of the honey or syrup. Before you seal the jar, say:
"Your friendship [or other appropriate word/s] *I have,*
By the power in me."

Repeat the full chant a few times before closing the lid securely.

"Sweetness keep and sweetness be / [words] *I have,*
By the power in me."

Hourly, daily or weekly (depending on the urgency) shake the bottle and repeat the chant.

When the spell is completed, return the ingredients to the earth, and wash out the jar, which you can reuse as you wish.

Freezer Spell

A freezer spell is a form of defensive or binding magic. In some ways, it is the opposite of the honey jar spell, which aims to improve interactions and relationships. A freezer spell, on the other hand, seeks to prevent – or freeze – negative behaviour or actions. Maybe you are the victim of gossip, or unscrupulous workplace activities and all other efforts to conciliate have failed. In this case, a freezer spell can be a handy addition to your Book of Shadows.

You will need:
- A container for the spell ingredients. The simplest container is a zip lock bag. Make sure your container is airtight and won't crack when frozen.
- Item/s linking to the situation, such as a photo, or description written on a piece of paper.
- Liquid, such as water, rotten milk or vinegar. Don't use alcohol, oil or cream as they don't freeze properly.
- Items to add to the liquid, such as salt, chilli, pepper or astringent herbs. Don't add your own body items or fluids to the container, as you don't want to form a personal link to a spell not meant for you.

Craft:
Add all items and liquid to your container. Seal the container and place in the freezer.

Over the next few hours, while the items begin to cool and freeze, use your creative imagination to see the impacts and consequences of your spell. You may like to remove the container from the freezer once or twice a week, allow to partially defrost, and then re-freeze it again while you focus on your aims.

When it's time to release the spellwork, remove it from the freezer. Flush the fluids down the toilet. Throw the other spell items into the wheely (rubbish) bin, as it is all just garbage now.

If your freezer is so packed with iced enemies that your ice-cream won't fit, it's time for a re-think: maybe it's not about 'them' but about you?

FLOURISH: The Circle Coven Tradition

The following section relates specifically to The Circle Coven tradition. It includes the foundations of our practice and shared approach to witchcraft. These glimpses into how a contemporary coven operates in an urban Australian context may be helpful as a guide if you are in the process of creating a new coven or would just like to know a bit more about coven life.

There are many valid ways to practice witchcraft. Here is just one pathway, that has been walked many times by members of The Circle Coven. It was blazed by occultists, witches, magicians and seers over thousands of years. The coven's tested and true practices provide signposts along this pathway. We know our practices work, because we have taken the journey, and returned to share the stories.

What is The Circle Coven?

The Circle Coven is the largest and longest running coven in Brisbane. It was founded in late 1999 by three witches who met in 1994, while they were members of an earlier training coven. Our coven roots draw nourishment from multiple sources including:

- ✦ **Wicca.** The Circle Coven hived off and evolved from the Coven of the Enchanted Cauldron, which was based on Alexandrian Wicca practices. However, 'eclectic' is the best descriptor for the current coven structure.
- ✦ *Hermeticism, chaos magic and ceremonial magick.*
- ✦ *Feminist spirituality.* For group harmony and stability, in 2007 we decided to accept only women into the coven. Coven members still continue to honour divine masculine energies in our rituals, and in everyday life we cherish interactions with fathers, sons, husbands, lovers, brothers, LGBTQIA+ friends and loved ones.
- ✦ *Western Initiatory and mystery traditions.* Within the coven, we focus on forming relationships with the divine. Members are not agnostic or atheist. Our structure integrates Initiations and rites of passage, which include the swearing of oaths.

> Coven members are like spokes in a wheel – none is first, none is last, and if one spoke collapses the whole wheel is destabilised.

The members of The Circle Coven tend to share some idiosyncrasies and norms. These aren't particularly magical in nature, but are central aspects of who we are and how we practice. For example, we don't take ourselves too seriously, and love to have a good laugh. However, we do take our magical practices and ritual work extremely seriously, as any Novice who has incorrectly drawn an invoking pentagram will confirm. In general, members hold progressive political views, such as endorsing universal access to healthcare, education and social support.

Significantly, Circle Coven members are mature in age, and most of the time we try to be mature in outlook. We aim to respond in a deliberate or inquisitive manner to things (and people) that oppose or annoy us, rather than react in an angry, knee-jerk way. Self-reflective, transformative practices are key aspects of our approach.

The way we do things
The Circle Coven has a vision statement, as we like to create a shared understanding of who we are, what we do and what we stand for:

Personal, spiritual and magical development within an experiential learning coven.

This means that all coven members have an individual responsibility to learn and develop:

- As a person. Transformations may occur through techniques such as shadow work or self-reflection.
- Spiritually. This refers to our relationship with deity.
- Magically. Magical development includes psychic abilities, spellwork, divination and ritual practices.

As well as a vision statement, The Circle Coven also has a set of principles and philosophical views. We feel these are integral to our practices as witches within The Circle Coven tradition. These include:

- *Celebrate the sabbats and esbats* to the best of your ability. These rituals help align you with the greater dance of life.
- *Nature* is the great teacher. The Earth is a living organism. Respect and honour Her.
- *Misery and joy* are self-created. Each is a decision, not a result. We all have the *responsibility* and ability to shape our lives.
- Be *honest* with yourself and others.
- *Physical world work*. Always consider the interrelationships between magical practice and 'real life'. You absolutely cannot ignore the physical for the many attractions of the spiritual realms. As the old saying goes: *'Trust in God but tether your camels.'* Stay grounded, pay your bills and keep it real. Most of the simple answers are found in the physical realm. Get enough sleep. Look after your body by eating moderate amounts of healthy food and exercise appropriately. Try to surround yourself with people who are

good for you and to you. Minimise contact with toxic people as much as you can.
- Work out what is *authentic* for you and grow towards this. Yes, this does mean discovering the masks or personas you frequently wear and the power of taking them off for a while and finding what is within.
- Own it. *You are accountable* for your own deeds and actions. Yes, sometimes it is the fault of other people. But ultimately, you are the one who can make the changes, as it's super difficult (if not impossible or irresponsible) to force other people to permanently change to your will. Do the work required to improve your life. A couple of crystals popped into your bra is not going to do this for you.
- *Boundaries*. Being a self-described empath with no control over how people's emotions influence you is not cool or desirable. Learn how to shield and create strong boundaries.
- "*Circle up, Witches*." Lean in, step up, and do the best you can.

The Circle Coven has a maximum of thirteen members at any one time. When there are too many witches in the group, we have noticed a tendency for coven members to split into mini-groups or factions. It is also difficult to keep interactions personal if the coven is too large. The limit on the number of members also takes into account practical considerations such as how to fit everyone into the ritual space and covensteads, where meetings are held.

We have a hierarchical system. The coven is led by two women who are the co-High Priestesses who are in turn supported by coven Elders. The Coven is not a democracy or run by 'majority rules' voting. Ultimately, the High Priestesses have final say ('veto') in the coven and how it operates, but this is usually done with consultation and input from members as much as possible. Coven members are welcome to query, challenge and question. In response, the High Priestesses aim to give honest explanations. However, sometimes it's simply not appropriate to discuss things at certain times; Initiation planning being a good example.

The Circle Coven doesn't agree with coveners being a member of another coven at the same time. This is due to magical 'leaks' between groups and the difficulties of working with similar, yet unalike, witchy energies. Also, we adopt an inward-looking focus, as coven members are our priority, rather than facing outwards to lead the local Pagan community in events or ceremonies. As a 'closed' coven, most of our lessons and rituals are for members only. That being said, The Circle Coven likes to maintain respectful and healthy relationships with other magical groups and practitioners.

A good coven is the opposite of a cult, because it is difficult to join, but easy to leave. If members choose to walk a different path, and resign from the coven at any stage, no one will stand in their way or hex them for their decision. If members no longer wish to be a part of the coven, we ask them to let one of the High Priestesses know and discuss their thoughts with them. We like to be upfront and let all our new starters know this, though it might seem strange to discuss resignation processes when beginning a new journey with a coven.

Our Probationary Novice (ProbNov) program

The Circle Coven only has Probationary Novice intakes every two years, to keep our membership stable. Taking on new members is a very big deal. However, over time, coven members relocate away from Brisbane or take on new responsibilities which need to be prioritised over coven commitments. When we get down to seven members, it's time to open up to new members.

When the coven is ready for a ProbNov intake, we advertise on witchy social media sites, and spread the word to friends in esoteric bookshops. Sometimes we approach witches we've met at events or interacted with on social media, and suggest they apply for membership. We then provide potential applicants with a copy of our 'Housekeeping' document (most of which has now been included in this book) as well as an application form. After the cut-off date, the High Priestesses scrutinise all the application forms, and thus begins the many staged approach to membership.

Unfortunately, not all applicants are offered a place in the Probationary Novice training. This could be due to minimal effort being put into completing the application form, or the witch's multiple competing priorities, travel distance or perceived 'fit' with the coven.

The next step is to invite those applicants who have made it through the first hoop (which is a massive step in itself) to an 'open night'. This meeting is an opportunity for the applicants to meet the coven members and other potential ProbNovs. Open nights can be so enjoyable. However, they can also be a nerve-wracking ordeal for applicants. For some attendees, this can be the very first time they've met other witches face-to-face, so it can be a watershed event.

All successful applicants undergo the Probationary Novice training program, regardless of their previous witchcraft knowledge or experience. This includes a mix of face-to-face lessons, self-directed learning, and independently submitting 'homework' activities within set timeframes. The emphasis is very much on the ProbNov doing the work required and attending all lessons.

On completion of the training program, ProbNovs may be offered a Novice position in the coven. Sometimes this is a perfect match between offer and expectations, but unfortunately this isn't always the case.

We don't charge money for Probationary Novice training. We never have, and we never will. It goes against our philosophy for witches to pay for coven training. Nor do we charge for rites of passage such as Dedications or Initiations. However, permanent coven members do contribute $50 a year towards coven funds. This covers venue hire as well as ritual and spellwork supplies. If we happen to end up with a surplus, it is donated to a carefully chosen local charity.

What do we look for in Probationary Novices?

- *Commitment, first and foremost.* Unlike an informal study group, coven activities are not optional, or 'when you feel like it' events. Consistent attendance at twice monthly events is a must. At the beginning of each year, we prepare a full calendar of ritual and lesson dates, so that members can forward plan.
- *Over the age of 30.* The decision to accept only people over the age of 30 has resulted in backlash from some younger folk who seek to join our coven. The main reason for the age limit is that current members are in their late 30s to 50s, so having members of a similar age promotes harmony. We like a foundation of harmony; in case you haven't noticed. Also, the years between 20 and 30 are busy, busy years. There's a lot of sudden and big changes going on during that decade of life. From more than 25 years of running covens, experience has shown that most members under the age of 30 don't tend to stick around. Nowadays we prefer stability over riotously changeable membership, so the over 30 years of age requirement is here to stay.
- *Privacy.* While some members are 'out of the broom closet', others are very private. We expect all members to avoid sharing details of other coveners without their specific agreement.
- *Attitude.* We like our members to be transparent in their communications, filled with curiosity and flexible in their responses to new opinions and learnings. We also treasure good manners and courtesy.
- *Distance.* Recently we added a proximity requirement. We prefer potential members to live within an hour of the covensteads located in Brisbane's

inner suburbs. We've found that, despite the very best of intentions, people find it difficult to travel over an hour each way at night to attend regular coven activities.

Rites of passage – Dedication and Initiation

The Circle Coven tradition has two key rites of passage, which are Dedication and Initiation. Initiation is a component in many ancient mystery schools and tribal societies. The Merriam Webster dictionary defines Initiations as:

> '…*the rites, ceremonies, ordeals, or instructions with which one is made a member of a sect or society…*'
> <www.merriam-webster.com/dictionary/initiation>

Initiation is therefore something conferred upon you within a group setting, rather than being a solitary activity. In addition, a particular degree or qualification in one coven does not necessarily have an equivalent in another group. This is why our training program for all new members starts at the beginner level, regardless of the witch's previous experience.

The Circle Coven's Initiatory degree system integrates archetypes relating to the Maiden, Mother, Crone and The Silent One. More information about these is included in the *Deity: Goddess, God and the Gods* chapter. Specific requirements need to be met before coveners are eligible for a rite of passage. Details of these have not been included in this publication, however giving or receiving sexual acts are not part of our Initiatory pathway.

This is The Circle Coven's usual pathway:

- Members start as a *Probationary Novice (ProbNov)*.
- They become a *Novice* when accepted as a coven member after successfully completing the training program.
- A year and a day after commencing training, Novices may approach the High Priestesses to request Dedication. Following a successful interview with the High Priestesses, members are known as a *Dedicatee*, in preparation for undertaking their Dedication ritual. The 'Dedicatee' term is specific to The Circle Coven. Yes, we made it up.
- After the Dedication ritual, the witch is known as a *Dedicant*. Dedicants are entitled to wear an athame in ritual.

✦ A minimum of a year passes between Dedication and Initiation – usually more. After Initiation, Circle Coven witches use a magical name and wear a special cord in ritual. They are known as *Initiate* or a *Priestess*.

For more information about what happens in The Circle Coven after Probationary Novice training, read *Living Witchery: Coven* by Alexandra Tanet. It's a great book, even if I do say so myself!

Preparing for Ritual

The section applies specifically to Circle Coven rituals, though of course concepts can be easily adapted for a solitary witch. For general information about solo or small group rituals, read the *Festivals: Rituals and Ceremonies* section.

Ritual clothing

Putting on a particular set of clothing to perform ritual or magical workings helps change your focus away from the mundane, towards the sacred. Clothing does influence how you feel and how you interact with others. While a discussion of attire and jewellery may seem trivial, on many other levels it is really quite important.

Some witches work skyclad (nude), preferring to have direct contact with nature. Nudity also means you have nothing to hide and everyone is equal in their fleshy forms. Aside from Initiations, or a rare ritual with the pre-arranged, willing consent of everyone, Circle Coven members wear red cotton robes.

You can tell the long-term coven members from newer members because the red dye fades over time with washing, from bright red to watermelon pink. Our robes are unadorned, and do not include a hood. They are made deliberately voluminous and baggy to allow unrestricted movement and decorous cross-legged sitting. We prefer ankle length robes which don't drag along the ground. Sleeves are relatively narrow to minimise the risk of catching a candle flame.

If you are a solitary witch, wear whatever you like.
Natural fibres are a better choice than synthetic fabrics for ecological reasons.

The Circle Coven arranges a group robe-making session for each intake of new Novices. Here, we impart wisdom such as *"do not cut the head hole too big"* and *"make sure the skirt isn't too tight."* The Circle Coven is fortunate to have an

Official Coven Seamstress, who provides us with handy guidance as we sew our robes, and bequeathed the knowledge about how to create linings.

It's easy to create a simple robe at home. Fold a length of material in half, with the cut edges together. The fold will form the shoulders and top of the sleeves. Lay a long and loose-fitting dress above the folded material, and draw around it to create an outline. The outline should be in the shape of a large 'T' with a flaring bottom. Make sure you allow for generous seams.

After marking out the T shape, cut away the bits under the sleeve down to the bottom of the material. Do not cut too much away the first time, as you can always trim in the sides later. Next, cut a hole for the head in the middle of the fold at the top. After the head hole is cut, then it's time to try on the oversized robe, before sewing a seam each side seam, along the underside of the sleeve right down to the bottom of the robe. You may like to sew your seams by hand, although in the coven we use sewing machines for speedy production.

How you wash your robes is up to you. I throw my robe into the washing machine with the family clothing, while other members prefer to hand wash their robe with salt. The main requirement is for robes to be clean and non-smelly for ritual.

Outer and underwear

When it's chilly, coveners wear a tight-fitting black skivvy (no cowl necks) and black leggings under their robes. For winter rituals, coveners add a cloak of their preferred design. Warmth should be prioritised over shiny panne velvet, no matter how pretty it looks. One of our members has a super toasty cloak which was a woollen blanket in its previous incarnation, and this works exceptionally well. We do not wear watches, hats, footwear (unless the ground is hazardous due to stones or uneven surfaces), or everyday underwear into a ritual.

Cords

The cord is nine foot long (2.7 m) and worn around the waist during ritual. It can be used for a handfasting ritual to entwine the bodies of the couple, or during binding spells or oaths. A tied cord represents the material plane linked to the spiritual planes. Within The Circle Coven, the colour of the cord also indicates the level or degree of the witch. Novices are initially given a silver cord to wear. Later, they make a plaited cord, which they are entitled to wear after Initiation.

Cords are knotted and worn in a specific way by coven members. The knot is *always* worn to the right side, because, according to our ex-High-Priest: *"The God is always right."* While that might be debateable, our cords are knotted at the right side of the body.

Jewellery

Within the coven, we ask members to consecrate their personal jewellery before wearing it in rituals. While many witches wear a pentagram pedant on a chain, you may like to keep some jewellery pieces separate and only wear them in ritual rather than each day. That way, when you don that item, it helps you move focus from the mundane to the sacred.

Getting ready

There are standard ways for preparing body and psyche for ritual within the coven. I find energy flows better during ritual if dedicated attention is given to preparations, so here's how coveners get ready.

Fasting

An empty stomach assists psychic work. For major or more demanding rituals such as Initiations, fast all day or longer. However, for the usual esbat or sabbat, have a light lunch, then don't eat anything more. After lunch, it's fine to drink fluids, including tea and coffee. In cases of low blood sugar, eating a small serve of nuts helps reduce light headedness. Of course, witches with diabetes or medical conditions require an individualised approach, so the above advice is general only.

Do not ingest large amounts of alcohol on the day of ritual, regardless of whether it is a coven or public ritual. I also advise against heavy drinking the night before a ritual and turning up hungover. Avoid ingesting non-prescription, mind-altering substances for at least seven days prior to ritual, unless required for that particular ritual. If we are of the Gods, and conduit for them, preparing a sound healthy body and mental space provides the best outcomes and experiences.

If you feel sick or are contagious with a cold or other virus, don't attend a close, intimate coven ritual – or a large, public group ritual either. However, if witches are just feeling low in energy, drained, or weary that's usually OK, as most people feel better after a ritual.

Ritually cleansing

Regardless of whether you are performing a ritual by yourself or with others, here's how to cleanse prior to ritual.

- ✦ Shower or bath and wash your hair.
- ✦ While washing yourself, place a small amount of salt into a cupped hand, add water and scrub your body. Visualise the water washing away the psychic grime of the day, and your aura and skin becoming clean and clear as you scrub.
- ✦ Consciously clear away any unpleasant thoughts or feelings and replace them with calm and uplifting thoughts.
- ✦ Use deodorant and/or antiperspirant. Antiperspirant is an *unofficial lesser tool* of The Circle Coven, as things can get quite sweaty in semi-tropical Queensland. I do not like to smell sweaty armpits. Strong-smelling perfume is also discouraged, due to the impacts on asthmatics or people with chemical sensitivities.
- ✦ Don't forget your mosquito repellent. This is another *unofficial lesser tool* of The Circle Coven, and we usually keep a spare bottle in the box of ritual supplies. Bugs will bite you regardless of how spiritually enlightened you consider yourself to be.
- ✦ Wearing makeup is fine, though certainly not compulsory. Hair is preferably worn loose or styled, rather than scrunched carelessly into a band.
- ✦ Stop thinking about mundane things. Don't worry about the boring and tedious aspects of life; think about the upcoming ritual. Reflect on the time of the year or moon phase or the working that you will be doing. Try to think pleasant, noncritical thoughts and speak kindly to all you meet, avoiding conflict.

Circle Coven Ritual

The following section steps through how The Circle Coven performs the opening and closing part of our esbat and sabbat rituals. With a bit of tweaking, it can be adopted to suit the solitary practitioner.

Preparations
- First things first. If required, remove twigs, rocks, or undesirable materials from the space to be used.
- Set up the altar with the necessary items and equipment.
- Meditate. The meditation differs, depending on how people are feeling on the night or the planned working. Usually, the coven prepares for ritual by toning specific sounds aligned to the body's energy points to help us centre and align. After the meditation, there is ritual silence and no idle chatter.
- Prepare the circle by:
  - Sweeping (or cleansing) the circle by psychically clearing with a besom or with your hands. This means moving around the space, releasing negative or stale energy by flinging it away to be transmuted and transformed.
  - Lighting the flares at each quarter (if used).
  - Lighting the charcoal blocks for the censor if these weren't lit in advance. Charcoal blocks can take a while to catch alight and we have a small set of tongs in our ritual box to prevent burnt fingers. Sprinkle some incense onto the block.
  - Lighting the Goddess and God candles while standing in front of the altar. First, light the Goddess candle using a taper, and then light the God candle.
- Anoint each person as they enter the circle. Place a pinch of salt into the oil bowl, and move to the entrance of the circle. As each person enters, dip your finger into the oil and trace a symbol (such as a pentagram) onto the forehead and wrists. Say *"In the names of the Goddess and the God, I bid*

you welcome to this their temple. Merry meet." We do not use herb bundles or smoking practices within the coven, and never have.

✦ When witches enter the circle (after being anointed and welcomed in) they stand in positions which are evenly spaced around the circle, with a few notable exceptions. No-one, unless they are performing a specific ritual function, stands behind the altar (which we have in the North). The areas in front of North, South, East and West are also left free so that welcoming and farewelling the quarters can occur smoothly.

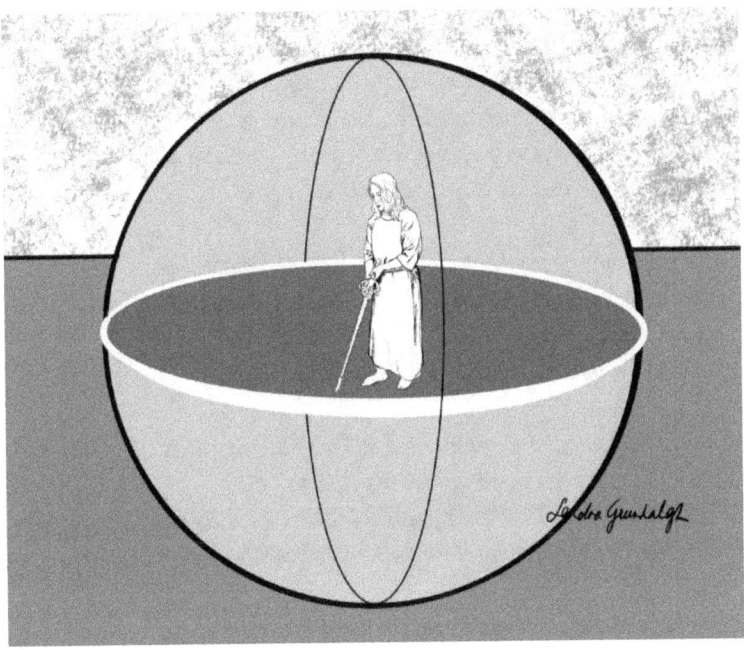

Circle casting

Cast the circle, beginning in the East quarter. We usually use the coven sword for this, but a wand or athame (or a stick) works just as well. First, salute the East by facing that direction and holding the sword with the pointy end up, high in front of you. Next, lower the sword so the tip is pointing towards the ground, though not touching. Walk around the edge of the circle in a clockwise direction, on the outside of all participants. Visualise the energy flowing through you and out of the sword tip.

As you walk, create an enormous etheric/astral bubble with its edge at the circumference of the circle. This is usually seen by the psychic senses as glowing white or bluey-white in appearance. Half of the sphere forms a dome above your head, the other half is below ground. As the circle cast occurs, the other witches lend their energy and visualisation focus to form a powerful protective orb.

The edge of a magical circle defines the different worlds, within and without. Within the circle is a safe and protected space. No beings of other realms can cause harm or distress inside a properly cast circle. Sometimes 'entities' or 'beings' outside the circle can be seen by the witches who are safely within – and that's where they should stay unless you deliberately invite them inside. You may experience significant changes of temperature when you exit a properly cast circle, or feel 'zinging' if you get too close to the boundary.

Circle cast technique poem
Find a place in hill or grove and feel the Goddess might.
Stand in the centre of your circle to be, and prepare your second sight.
Close your eyes and form a light in a ball, that starts down low.
In the base is where it starts, let your body feel it grow.

Draw it up through your heart and down your arm quite slow.
As the light builds up, and you feel you'll burst, it's time to let it go.
Through hand, or wand, or blade or sword, direct it ever down.
Begin to move and visualize the light upon the ground.

We say the chant, and concentrate our will with all our might,
Round and round, deosil we cast the magic light.
When end meets start still say the words be sure to join the two,
Pause and regain your energies for there's only one more thing to do.

Move back to the centre again and see your border shining,
Close your eyes and use your will to create the protective lining.
Up and up you draw the sides that look like polished chrome,
Up and up you draw the light till at last you're in a dome.
(DS)

After the circle cast, strengthen the circle boundary by rounds of censing and asperging. One witch adds salt to the bowl of water on the altar, saying a set of words. They then walk to the East quarter and wait there. A second witch adds incense to the charcoal on the altar to summon Fire and Air, once again saying certain wording. After that, they join the witch waiting in the East. One after the other, they walk just inside the boundary of the circle, sprinkling salted water while the incense smoke wafts.

Once the circle is cast, participants stay within the bounds of the circle. If anyone needs to leave urgently, they quietly speak to the High Priestess/s or an experienced covener. We then create a doorway in the circle to allow the person to exit in a magically appropriate manner, and one of the coveners goes with them to provide support if required. If participants feel really strange or dizzy during a coven ritual, our advice is to let an experienced covener know straight away, so we can offer the appropriate assistance.

Quarters

Call the quarters, one at a time, to welcome the energy of the elements. Stand at the edge of the circle, facing outwards to the pertinent direction. Intone the words, rather than speaking with a normal voice. Here are our coven's calls for each direction:

East: *"Breeze light, airy flight. Powers old, we call thee."*
South: *"Flame ablaze, sunny days. Powers old, we call thee."*
West: *"Waters sweet, oceans deep. Powers old, we call thee."*
North: *"Stone still, earthy hill. Powers old, we call thee."*
Centre: *"Spirit bright, starry sight. Powers old, we call thee."*

All coven members join in with the shared refrain of: *"Powers old, we call thee."*

Then, draw an invoking pentagram, no higher than your head, no lower than your waist. Within the coven, we use an invoking (and banishing) pentagram of Earth. Hold your finger/athame up towards your head, and sweep it down towards your left hip (with your arm held straight) to make the first side of the pentagram. Next, sweep up your arm towards your right shoulder, then across to your left shoulder, down towards your right hip and back to the starting point at head height.

There's a funny little movement you make at each point, subtly twisting your hand so the blade of your athame is held in a slicing direction. If you are using your finger, hold your hand so your palm is kept in a downward position. Visualise a white pentagram glowing in the air in front of you.

To complete the invoking pentagram process, bring your finger or athame to your lips, as if you are telling someone to be quiet. This action is known as the *Sign of Silence*.

Finally, light the candle for that quarter. We keep a lit taper ready for this purpose.

Invocation and evocation

Invite the presence of the Goddess and God into the circle. Most of the time, we use an evocation, rather than an invocation during our rituals.

An *evocation* (bringing forth) is when the energies of the divine are invited into the ritual space and everyone partakes of these. An *invocation* (bringing in) occurs when deity is ecstatically channelled into one or more specific people during a ritual. We include either an invocation or an evocation, but not both in the same ritual.

During an evocation to Goddess, all coveners position themselves with legs wide and arms stretched sideways at shoulder height, so we stand in the shape of a star. One witch says the following words, evoking the divine feminine into the circle:

> *Beloved Goddess. Mother of all things.*
> *Lady of the green fields and shining moon.*
> *You have been known by many names.*
> *You are Hecate, Anu, Persephone, Diana.*
> *You are sister, mother, lover and daughter.*
> *You are the beauty within us all.*
> *We adore thee.*
> *Be with us this night.*

For the evocation of the divine masculine, coveners stand with legs together, clenched fists and arms crossed over chest. This stance is similar to statues depicting the Egyptian god Osiris. One witch says:

> *Beloved God. Father of all things.*
> *Horned one of the fields, green man of the forest.*
> *You have been known by many names.*

You are Beli, Apollo, Cernunnos, Pan.
You are brother, father, lover and son.
You are the strength that is within us all.
We adore thee.
Be with us this night.

For invocations, a witch allows their personality to 'step aside' so a particular goddess or god can temporarily dwell within them. This is called Drawing Down the Moon. Current coven practice during invocations includes speaking *The Charge of the Goddess*, which was originally created by Gerald Gardner and Doreen Valiente.

That's the ritual setup done. Now it's down to business.

Magical working

During this part of the ritual the coven collectively performs a spell, healing, consecration or dramatic re-enactment. At times, the witch who prepares the working keeps part of it a secret. On other occasions, everyone is involved well in advance.

A magical working during ritual consists of:
1. Preparing the items required for the working
2. Raising energy, by chanting or movement
3. Channelling the energy
4. Releasing the energy at its peak (usually someone is nominated to call 'down!')
5. Grounding excess energy.

> Each time a witch says "*So mote it be*" during a ritual, everyone repeats it back. This phrase serves as a focus point, to facilitate ritualists sending their energies towards the outcome, so that things will occur as desired. It also marks an end point to confirm that the action is complete.

Cakes and ale

'Cakes and ale' occurs after the magical working is completed. This ritual component is also known as the symbolic great rite, or sacred marriage. While we know paths to generative and creative union are not confined to duality of gender or sex, this is standard coven practice. Ceremoniously blessing and then sharing food and drink marks a more relaxed part of the ritual and assists us to ground.

The name 'cakes and ale' is an artefact from our old coven. The Circle Coven has never used ale and rarely includes cakes. The fluid is usually mead or port, and for cakes we share biscuits, rice crackers or apple slices. Round biscuits with white icing (readily available from supermarkets) are a nice option, as they symbolise the full moon.

The food and fluid for 'cakes and ale' is ritually prepared by two witches, one holding the vessel, and the other using their athame or hand to bless and charge the substances. The chalice and platter are then passed around the circle from person to person. Coveners are expected to drink from the same chalice, however, if anyone has a contagious condition, they bring their own cup into the ritual or perform a libation instead. A libation ceremoniously returns drink and food to the earth.

Closing the sacred space.

After 'cakes and ale', close down the circle quickly and without fuss. Thank and farewell the Goddess and God. This is usually done by the witches who performed the evokes. Next, farewell the quarter guardians, changing the words of the chant to *"We thank thee"* instead of *"We call thee."* Draw a banishing pentagram (see image below), and then pinch out the quarter candle.

To banish, start with your finger/athame held in front of you, near your left hip. Sweep up towards your head, down towards your right hip, up to your left shoulder, across to your right shoulder and finish where you started, near your left hip.

By the way, when you call upon the Gods or invite the quarters in a ritual they do not really 'go away' when you farewell them. They are always there, but you are closing off your access and awareness of them. However, it is easier for us to visualise them returning to their magical realms and leaving us behind.

After that, the witch who cast the circle steps forward and breaks the magical boundary by thrusting the sword through it. They declare:

"The circle is open but unbroken!"

This is the cue for everyone to link arms and dance around with great enthusiasm, while singing a song to mark the end of the ritual.

It's now time to clean the ritual gear, tip the remnants from the censor onto the paving stones and pack everything back into the storage box. Finally, we share food and drink and chat about the ritual and anything else that comes to mind.

Our magical work is done.

References and Bibliography

Buckland, Raymond, *Buckland's Complete Book of Witchcraft*, Llewellyn Publications: USA, 1986 (1997 version)
Crowley, Aleister. *Magick, Liber ABA: Book IV*, Red Wheel/Weiser; 2nd Revised ed. Edition, 2005
Cunningham, Scott, *Cunningham's Encyclopedia of Magical Herbs*, Llewellyn Publications: USA, 1985
Cunningham, Scott, *Wicca: Magic for the Solitary Practitioner*, Llewellyn Publications: USA, 1993
Farrar, Janet and Stewart, *A Witches Bible Compleat*, Phoenix Publishing
Fenton, Sasha, *Super Tarot*, The Aquarian Press, 1991
Fortune, Dion, *The Sea Priestess*, The Aquarian Press, 1989
Fortune, Dion, *The Cosmic Doctrine*, Weiser edition, 2000
Hutton, Ronald, *The Stations of the Sun*, Oxford University Press, 1996
Mooney, Thorn, *Traditional Wicca*, Llewellyn Worldwide
Starhawk, *The Earth Path: Grounding Your Spirit in the Rhythms of Nature*, HarperCollins: USA, 2006
Starhawk, *The Spiral Dance: A Rebirth of the Ancient Religion of the Great Goddess*, Harper & Row: USA, 1979
Tanet, Alexandra, *Living Witchery: Coven*, Byrning Tyger, 2001
White, Marie, *Mary-el Tarot*, Schiffer Publishing: USA, 2012.

Additional Resources for Further Study

Antipodean Arts – podcast
Australian Pagan Awareness Network (PAN) – trusted Aussie Pagan info site
Australian Witchcraft – Facebook group
Billinghurst, Frances, *Dancing the Sacred Wheel*, Createspace
Experience Tarot Magic – online class with Mary K. Greer, located on this site:
   <globalspiritualstudies.com/product/experience-tarot-magic/>
Kraig, Donald Michael, *Modern Magick: Twelve Lessons in the High Magickal Arts*, Llewellyn Publications: USA, 2010
Greenhalgh, Sandra & White, Elkie (editors), *A History of Druidry in Australia*, Byrning Tyger
Herb Rally – herbal monographs, which can be found on this site:
   <https://www.herbrally.com/monographs>
K, Amber, *Coven Craft: Witchcraft for Three or More*, Llewellyn Worldwide
Meredith, Jane, *Circle of Eight: Creating Magic for Your Place on Earth*, Llewellyn Worldwide
Pinkola Estes, Clarissa, *Women Who Run with the Wolves*, Ballantine Books
Plant.net – plant identification app
Ravenwolf, Silver, *To Stir a Magic Cauldron: A Witch's Guide to Casting and Conjuring* Llewellyn Publications: USA, 2005
Ticknel, Alawn, *The Shamanistic Wheel of the Year. A Manual for Wise Shapers or Personal Growth & Development Through the Seasons*, Pagan Products Publications: Galdraheim Coven, 1987
Witches + Pagans of Queensland – Facebook group
Witches Workshop – Facebook group
Witch: Radiant and Rooted – podcast.

Disclaimer: unashamed bias has been applied when choosing some of the Australian-based resources.

Acknowledgements and Credits

Thanks so much you awesome people!

- Tess Hudson for editorial support, fact checking, trying to steer us clear of political rocks of doom, and her sage advice and words.
- Gillian, Jill, Marilyn and Kerri for beta reading.
- Linda Marson for her amazing grammatical know-how and diligence.
- Melissa May for letting us use her chant.
- Luke from FleetFoot Photography for the back cover image.
- Jae Arnell for the Djuit image
- Kim Fairminer for moon cycles diagram
- A'Rowan for the Wheel of the Year image
- Sandra Greenhalgh for other interior images, inspired by photos by:
    - Ki'ian – Festivals page
    - Adam Bolt Photography – Foundations page
    - FleetFoot Photography – Fundamentals, Flourish and final
    - Scarlet Paige – Focus page.

Biographies

Alexandra Tanet
Alexandra Tanet is the nom de plume for a Brisbane witch who prefers to keep a low profile on electronic and social media. She cast her first spell as a teenager and has been involved in leading covens for over 25 years. Alexandra is currently co-High Priestess of The Circle Coven.

Alexandra is the primary author of *Living Witchery: Coven*, the first book in the *Living Witchery* series. She is delighted to write and co-edit *Living Witchery: Beginner Witch Guide* with support from friends of The Circle Coven.

Kim Fairminer
Kim is an astrologer, writer, and witch with more than 20 years hands-on experience as a magical practitioner. She has been a member of The Circle Coven for over 10 years, including six years in the role of High Priestess. Before her life-changing midlife transits, she was an editor for a multinational company. She writes horoscopes and forecasts for a range of publications and shares esoteric wisdom on the *Witch: Radiant + Rooted* podcast. Kim writes, stargazes, and circle-casts from her home in suburban Brisbane.

You can learn more about her work at kimfairminer.com.

Sandra Greenhalgh
Sandra is an author, artist and occultist who lives in Brisbane, Australia. A long-term participant, student and teacher of Western Mystery traditions, she joined The Order of Bards, Ovates and Druids in 1988, while working in England and Europe.

Growing up in the Queensland countryside helped foster her deep love of the wild places of bush, beach and the outback. Whenever possible, Sandra retreats to camping beside the ocean with her extended family and friends.

Sandra has over 30 years of Neopagan community involvement. Tarot and divination are passions, and in 2019 Sandra created a new deck of oracle cards focussing on Druidic lore, called the *Druid Wisdom Oracle*. She also authored the *Druid Wisdom Oracle Guidebook*, released in 2020.

In 2020, Sandra co-edited *A History of Druidry in Australia*, which includes contributions from over thirty Australians who practice Druidry.

Sandra is grateful to live with her husband, two teenage children and a couple of spoilt cats. Between writing, drawing and procrastinating, she works in healthcare.

See byrningtyger.com for more information.

A'Rowan

A'Rowan is a Brisbane based creative who was summoned to the Craft by the power of fragrance. Deity and myth-based perfumes from Ancient Egypt, Greece and Rome started an intangible access into other realms using the alchemy of essences as their guide. These fragrances are portals into mediative states and magick.

Deep engagement with the visual world and shared creative work sustains A'Rowan, as does her coven life. A'Rowan is currently immersed in the beauty of Theban text and dreams of Glastonbury.

Chadrac Sloane

I am a proud Barkindji woman and I have walked a spiritual path for my whole life thanks to the teachings of my family Elders. My practice is of an eclectic nature but is deeply rooted in the traditional knowledge that has been entrusted to me. I am a mother, a grandmother, and a worshipper of nature.

I have worked in many occupations over the years but always remained present in my practice. My real first job after leaving school early in Year Ten was as a dental nurse. That did not last long as I promptly realised I needed to be out amongst the natural environs. This saw me packing up and fully changing direction in occupation, by heading off to work the harvest seasons. This involved traveling the agricultural belts of the Nation, chasing the in-season fruit and veggies, so to speak.

Many years on from this and several children later, now at an age where labouring is no longer physically pleasant, I moved back into semi-inside desk work. I enrolled at University as a mature-age student to complete a Bachelor of Arts in sociology and criminology. Moving forward, I am working on further postgraduate study and research that will benefit Indigenous communities.

Jacq Hackett
At the height of her career as an elite real estate professional, coven member Jacq was sought out to share the secret of her success. The properties she serviced sold faster, for more money and with happier clients than those of her peers. Her guest speaker appearances at interstate business seminars and subsequent interview on *Real Estate Experts* caught the attention of industry coaches worldwide.

While the corporate world accepts certain 'New Age' practices such as the law of attraction, Jacq introduced a unique twist as the only internationally recognised witch in real estate, using the psychology of ancient witchcraft in modern business.

To date, Jacq has shared her knowledge of energy realignment and cleansing via her online and published works, a short documentary produced by Queensland University of Technology and as an active member within the Australian and international Pagan community.

Ki-ian
Ki-ian is an earth lover, herbalist and practitioner of embodied witchcraft who has her feet firmly planted in the soil.

Spending her childhood weaving between her family home in the suburban outskirts of Sydney and the east coast bushlands, it was here Ki-ian's first learnt to sit in stillness listening to the cadence of nature observing her rhythm and flow.

In her on-farm apothecary she creates products deeply grounded in ritual with mindfully grown herbs, harvested to meet the needs of the magic. This manifests in the form of practical magic where essential oils, herbs and hydrosols are brewed into offerings that offer awakening to pleasure and purpose.

Ki-ian facilitates workshops and invites 1:1 internships where she teaches all aspects of matter to magic with a focus on regeneration, earth care and connection to country from which the matter is harvested.

For more information, visit solumfarm.com/witchesapothecary

Merewyn
Merewyn's interest in the craft began when her grandmother introduced her to palmistry and tea-leaf reading in the 1960s. It wasn't until her late 30s that she discovered a teaching coven where she started her journey in earnest. It

was an intense and sometimes challenging journey, a place of learning, self-discovery and the making of long friendships. It was here she met Alexandra, Scarlet and Rhianna, who would have a profound influence on the direction of her witch-life.

Merewyn was a founding member of SAW Coven with Alexandra and Scarlet and spent a few years as coven incense maker, teaching students, working with the coven in rotating roles as Maiden or High Priestess, writing rituals and lessons. However just before she turned 50, Merewyn succumbed to a bout of glandular fever and stepped back from the coven to recoup. She currently resides with her cat in a cosy home just outside Brisbane where her neighbours sometimes wonder about the funny noises coming from her garden around the full moon.

Scarlet Paige
Scarlet Paige is a 50-something woman who is in love with life and considers herself a 'bit of a hippie'. She is a child of the Earth who fell in love with everything and anything occult in her teen years and has never stopped searching and learning.

Scarlet is currently High Priestess as well as one of the founding members of The Circle Coven. She dabbled in various spiritual practices and in her twenties joined a Brisbane Bayside Coven where she embraced witchcraft in all its aspects. Scarlet is an empath and a balanced practitioner of the craft, with a love of intricate rituals and spell work. In her mundane life, Scarlet is an educator of young minds, partner and mother of two. Scarlet lives in Brisbane but yearns to move to the seaside.

www.ingramcontent.com/pod-product-compliance
Lightning Source LLC
Chambersburg PA
CBHW050307010526
44107CB00055B/2145